# THE HOUSEHOLD ENDOWMENT MODEL

WEALTH PLANNING
*for*
AFFLUENT FAMILIES

# THE HOUSEHOLD ENDOWMENT MODEL

VINCE ANNABLE

This book is for general informational purposes only and is not intended to provide, and may not be relied upon as providing, client-specific investment advice. Any such advice would require a detailed understanding of a particular client's investment profile, which is beyond the scope of this work.

- Nothing in the book should be viewed as investment advice or an investment recommendation.
- Investments involve risk and may result in loss.
- The strategies in the book are not suitable for all investors, and investments should be discussed with a qualified investment professional.
- Any potential tax implications should be discussed with a qualified tax attorney or an accountant.

WEALTH **STRATEGIES**
ADVISORY GROUP

THE HOUSEHOLD ENDOWMENT MODEL
*Wealth Planning for Affluent Families*

ISBN   978-1-5445-0235-9 *Paperback*
      978-1-5445-0236-6 *Ebook*

*This book is dedicated to my father and mother, Robert and Madelon Annable, who told me my entire life growing up that I could achieve anything I set my mind to, and to my wife, Deborah, and our five children, Matthew, Robert, Lauren, Jonathon, and Katelyn, because they always stuck with me in every pursuit of those goals and dreams. My wife never quit believing in me and to this day is my biggest supporter.*

*And...*

*To our many faithful clients, who believed in me and The Household Endowment Model and trusted me with their hard-earned assets.*

*And...*

*To my team, Aaron, Lauren, JT, Andrew Dinkelmeyer, and Talia, who have supported and worked tirelessly in the growth of The Household Endowment Model.*

# CONTENTS

# INTRODUCTION

Remember 2008? Who could possibly forget the market collapse that led to the Great Recession? Perhaps by that point you had already suffered through the 2001 dot-com bubble-burst.

Even after those tumultuous times, many people are still riding the stocks-and-bonds roller coaster. It can be difficult to SWAN—Sleep Well At Night—with a portfolio of potentially volatile investments. Imagine how much better you would sleep if you knew your assets were in a portfolio that wasn't totally correlated to stocks and bonds and the volatility that comes with them and could potentially both maintain and increase your wealth.

You're about to learn how to do this. Get ready to learn how to invest and manage your family's wealth in such a way that you might well generate higher total returns, lower risk, stabilize portfolio volatility, and realize your financial goals.

## THE ROLLER COASTER

At the turn of the millennium, investors were euphoric. As the still-novel internet grew, tech companies—"dot-coms"—with extremely high valuations proliferated. Everyone was jumping on board. It seemed like you could throw a dart at *The Wall Street Journal* investment section and hit a winner. Everything was going up, and everyone, motivated by FOMO, "fear of missing out," wanted a piece of the action and expected hyper-returns. Fear and greed both had their parts in making the market surge to all-time highs.

Then the tech bubble burst. After the market meltdown, investors rushed for the exits, trying to save what they had left. Savings were obliterated, retirement plans were delayed, and college expenses were put on hold.

The economy and market eventually recovered. In 2005, things started to take off again. The market roller coaster climbed precipitously, surpassing old highs and reaching new ones. The residential real estate market in particular broke all records. If you could fog a mirror, you could finance any number of properties without putting up a dime of equity. In many cases, you could receive 110 percent or more of the property's appraised value. Lenders were now paying you to take on more debt.

Investors flipped properties at lightning speed. The press ran stories about grandmothers buying and immediately flipping multiple homes in Florida, California, and Arizona. You couldn't go to a bridge club or a bar without getting real estate advice. FOMO and the lust for hyperreturns once again sent markets higher and higher. Fear and greed were taking hold...again.

In 2008, the music suddenly stopped, and many people found themselves with nowhere to sit. The chairs were pulled out from under not only individual investors but banks, financial institutions, and the global economy. The sky had fallen, and the world was coming to an end! The biggest names on Wall Street were failing or receiving government bailouts to prevent economic collapse. A new term, the *Great Recession*, was on everyone's lips.

It was under these circumstances that I began an intensive search to find a better way for my clients to invest. I discovered the primary culprit for investor grief was lack of diversification. All, or most, investment portfolios looked the same: 60 percent stocks and 40 percent bonds, or variations on that basic theme. All or most of these investments were correlated. In other words, they moved in unison. When the market raced to the top, everything climbed along with it. When the market dropped, everyone jumped out at the same time.

## AN ALTERNATIVE INVESTMENT MODEL

My search for a solution led me to Yale University's Endowment Fund and the endowment model created by its chief investment officer, David Swensen. You'll learn much more about this investment model in the first part of this book. For the moment, suffice it to say that Swensen's model was significantly, even massively, outperforming conventional markets. It reduced exposure to domestic public stocks and bonds and diversified through private "alternative investments."

When I discovered it in 2010, the Yale Endowment Model was an alternative-investment-based-model portfolio that consisted largely of private investments in noncorrelated assets managed by best-of-class outside managers. These private investments were alternatives to the publicly traded markets, and since they were investments in private assets, they were not subject to the violent ups and downs of the public market roller coaster. The genius part was Swensen's insistence that outside managers—managers not directly employed by Yale and its Endowment Fund—handle each category of investment. These managers were specialists who had proven themselves in their respective asset classes.

My goal was to find a way to create a similarly diversified, non-correlated investment strategy for individuals and families, enabling them to make private, institutional-style investments with minimums in the $50,000 to $100,000 range rather than in the millions. The investment model that resulted would be made up of a number of classes of both private and public investments, each managed by best-of-class outside managers. This led me to create the Wealth Strategies Advisory Group and its unique wealth-management strategy: The Household Endowment Model, or THEM for short. I'll share this strategy with you in the pages that follow.

THEM is primarily designed for affluent, high-net-worth families and individuals—or those who want to be—who have only recently been empowered to make institutional-style, non-correlated private investments. Unfortunately, this investment model is one that very few of these people know about.

Based on our experience of reviewing the prior investments of new clients, which typically show primarily stocks and bonds, this is in large part because many of their investment counselors have no idea these strategies and opportunities exist and typically don't have access to them. Many of our new clients ask us why this type of investment strategy was never mentioned or offered by prior advisors. One of THEM's critical components is access to the professionals who manage these private investments.

While institutional-style investments are a cornerstone of THEM, they are just one of several pillars of this overall wealth-management strategy. In fact, the strategy addresses all five of the primary concerns most high-networth families contend with.

These concerns include the following:

1. Wealth Preservation: Investment consulting to maximize the probability of achieving financial goals. This is where institutional-style investing enters the picture.
2. Wealth Enhancement: After the family investment portfolio is stabilized, attention shifts to mitigating tax liability while helping ensure the family has the cash flow it needs. Paying less in taxes leaves more money to be invested, helping these families meet more of their financial goals.
3. Wealth Transfer and Estate Planning: The smoothest, most tax-efficient way to pass on assets to loved ones and intended heirs.
4. Wealth Protection/Asset Protection: Protecting accumulated wealth from creditors, litigants, potential lawsuits, and catastrophic loss.
5. Charitable Giving: Fulfilling charitable goals in the

ways most beneficial to their families and the causes they care about.

THEM and its overall wealth-planning strategy have been designed to cover all five of these bases.

The Household Endowment Model was also created for entrepreneurs and successful business owners—high-net-worth individuals, perhaps like yourself, whose attention is focused on their businesses, where their assets are tied up. You often have neither the bandwidth nor expertise to manage your net worth in ways that are designed to both mitigate risk and maximize your wealth and business assets.

You are probably building your business to the point where it can be sold profitably. That's your retirement plan and your legacy. However, proper planning can't wait until the day before you decide to sell. If you don't want to give up most of the profit from selling your business to the taxman, you should plan for the sale five to ten years before it happens.

Nor do you want to create a successful business only to have a nuisance lawsuit or similar catastrophe take it away from you. Once your business has stabilized, we advise you to diversify and transfer your wealth and assets from your business to your personal estate with guidance from tax and legal professionals. Protecting the value of your business and its assets involves planning and executing an intricate transition process. The Household Endowment Model offers solutions to all of these challenges.

## THE WAY FORWARD

To address the specific needs and primary concerns of high-net-worth individuals and families, this book has been divided into two parts. The first part deals with the first pillar of THEM: the theory and practice behind alternative, non-correlated investment strategies, and how high-net-worth individuals and families can now take advantage of them. Much of what you read in this section has come from the strategies I have gleaned from Yale, other endowment funds, and many of the top institutional investors, such as Blackstone. These strategies are not new but have been adapted to The Household Endowment Model for the benefit of our clients.

The second part discusses the remaining four pillars of the model: wealth enhancement, wealth transfer and estate planning, wealth protection/asset protection, and—since a large percentage of affluent families want to give back—charitable giving.

It's difficult to SWAN—Sleep Well At Night—when your financial future is uncertain. By the time you finish putting the strategies in this book into practice, you'll be able to rest easy, with the knowledge that your family's financial future is potentially more secure, no matter what future swings the economy might have in store.

I always say, "When it comes to investing, your money doesn't come with instructions." Think of this book you are about to read as your money manual, with a set of instructions to help guide you in managing your money, assets, and legacy. Let's get started.

## PART I

# THE HOUSEHOLD ENDOWMENT MODEL: WHAT AND WHY

# CHAPTER 1

# THE MARKET'S— AND YOUR—UPS AND DOWNS

Do you remember where you were and how you were feeling in September 2008? Of course you do.

That's like asking people alive at the time if they remember where they were when JFK was assassinated or when the first men landed on the moon. Do you remember where you were on September 11, 2001?

The years 2008 to 2009 were the worst market meltdown and financial crash since the Great Depression. Everything fell apart in September 2008.

## WHAT HAPPENED?

The causes of the Great Recession will be endlessly discussed and debated. When the housing bubble, with its rampant speculation, burst, the dominoes rapidly fell.

A few representative facts and figures paint a vivid picture of the collapse:

- In 2008, the US stock market lost approximately 40 percent of its value and declined 55 percent from its high on October 9, 2007, to its low on March 6, 2009.[1]
- That year, the average equity mutual fund lost almost 40 percent of its value.[2]

---

1   Standard & Poor's, "S&P Equity Indices Fact Sheet," December 31, 2009. Note: Market closing value peak on October 9, 2007, was 1,565.15. Market closing value bottom was on March 9, 2009, at 676.53. Percentage loss of 55.38 percent does not include dividends.

2   https://www.marketwatch.com/story/hedge-fund-like-mutual-funds-bid-for-your-money-2010-03-19 and https://money.usnews.com/money/blogs/new-money/2009/01/07/if-your-stock-fund-lost-less-than-38-in-2008-youre-gold.

- In 2009, the market declined another 26 percent before beginning to recover.[3]
- The average 401(k) retirement plan lost a quarter of its value in 2008.[4]

This was a real killer. People who were getting ready to retire in 2008 all of a sudden had to put their dreams on hold. Some of these people had already put off retirement when the dot-com bubble burst in 2001–2002.

More broadly, the Great Recession affected almost every investor and the economy as a whole. The underlying problem was the monkey-see-monkey-do investment strategy that permeated the markets. Most investment portfolios looked and acted the same: 60 percent stocks and 40 percent bonds. They still do.

The publicly traded stocks that make up about 60 percent of most portfolios are, almost by definition, correlated to the market and its ups and downs. When the markets move up, the stocks in your portfolio move up, which feels great. When the markets move down, your stocks go down, which feels like you felt in 2008—terrible.

---

3    On March 6, 2009, the S&P 500 fell to an intraday low of 666.79. *The RIC Report, Investment Strategy*, Bank of America Merrill Lynch, March 11, 2010, p. 1.

4    Tiburon Research, *Key Driving Factors: Defining the Role of Consumer Wealth, the Institutional Markets, and Current Events in the Future of Advice*, March 2010, p. 9.

The market is a roller coaster, as this illustration of its ups and downs in the last twenty-five years shows, and you need to get off.

Why Alternative Investments?

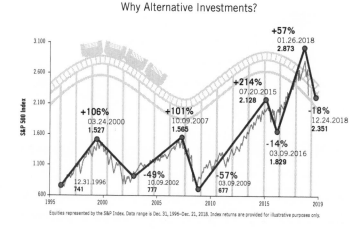

Equities represented by the S&P Index. Data range is Dec. 31, 1996–Dec. 21, 2018. Index returns are provided for illustrative purposes only.

Do you feel like you've been riding this roller coaster since 1996? That's because if you're a typical individual investor, you have been.

The market's bumpy ride gets investors to make emotional decisions. In a downturn, people get hysterical and say to themselves, "Let's sell and save what's still left!" This is not always the right move. By the end of 2009, the market eventually posted a 26.5 percent gain from its admittedly dismal showing on January 1, but the gain came too late for those who had sold in a panic. They had sold at the worst possible time.

The emotional decisions made when markets are crashing and investors exit create a new problem. When do you get back into the market? The Household Endowment Model's goal is to build a portfolio of publicly traded and alternative, non-traded investments to help smooth out this roller-coaster ride.

In 2008, professionals reacted, or were forced to react, much as average-Joe and average-Jane investors did. As Daniel Wildermuth of Kalos Financial puts it, "During this downfall, much of the downward pressure on the markets resulted from professionals unloading their holdings. The world's largest banks and hedge funds often sold at huge losses at the worst possible time to deleverage their balance sheets. They needed cash at all costs just when cash was the most expensive." This also happened to mutual funds that were required to be fully invested. They had to liquidate their portfolios to raise the cash needed for the liquidations.

Bond markets, which comprise about 40 percent of the typical portfolio, are correlated to interest rates. When interest rates go up, bond values go down. The truth is that bonds haven't necessarily been a good investment since the long-ago bull market of the '80s. This chart proves the point:

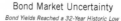

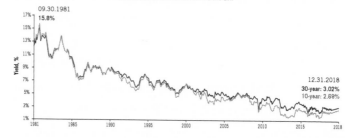

Yet investment advisors still regularly put 40 percent of their clients' assets in bonds.

The truth is that the 15.8 percent return on bonds received in 1981 came at a time when inflation was around 10.35 percent, according to the US Bureau of Labor Statistics Consumer Price Index (CPI). The inflation of the late '70s and early '80s created a huge bull market in bonds, since bonds gain value when interest rates go down and lose value when interest rates go up.

Bonds purchased during inflationary times become more valuable during times of deflation, so the '80s and '90s were a good time to buy bonds. However, since interest rates may now be at an all-time low, an investment in bonds certainly has the potential to lose value when interest rates increase—as they are poised to do.

The '80s and '90s also saw a bull market in stocks, which grew in value along with bonds. Since we are now potentially near a stock market peak, stocks purchased at this point are almost certain to go down in value as the market declines.

While the 60/40 model may have worked in the past, you may now need to diversify. To get off the roller coaster, your investments should not be entirely correlated to either publicly traded markets, like stocks, or interest rates, like bonds. You need alternatives to the typical correlated investments. Fortunately, help is on the way.

## WANTED: A NEW STRATEGY

Times change, and sometimes for the better. Look at this ad as an example:

According to repeated nationwide surveys,

# More Doctors Smoke CAMELS than any other cigarette!

**Doctors in every branch of medicine were asked, "What cigarette do you smoke?" The brand named most was Camel!**

You'll enjoy Camels for the same reasons so many doctors enjoy them. Camels have cool, cool *mildness*, pack after pack, and a *flavor* unmatched by any other cigarette.

Make this sensible test. Smoke only Camels for 30 days and see how well Camels please your taste, how well they suit your throat as your steady smoke. You'll see how enjoyable a cigarette can be!

**THE DOCTORS' CHOICE IS AMERICA'S CHOICE!**

*For 30 days, test Camels in your "T-Zone" (T for Throat, T for Taste).*

Those of you old enough to remember when this sort of thing was legal probably just let out an ironic chuckle. Those who aren't may have just felt their jaws drop to the floor. These days, doctors would never recommend smoking—or even vaping! If they did, they'd risk losing their licenses.

However, investment advisors and brokers can, and still do, recommend the standard 60/40 portfolio. A 2013 PerTrac/Dalbar study, the latest available, showed the average investor in the prior twenty years had an average annual return of 2.5 percent, the Standard & Poor's (S&P) index an 8 percent return, and private investments a return of 15 percent. Those private investments were typically non-traded, illiquid, alternative investments in venture capital or private equity. This is illustrated in the following chart:[5]

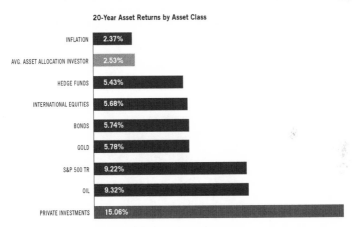

Investors' Emotional Decisions Often Cause Underperformance

**20-Year Asset Returns by Asset Class**

|  |  |
|---|---|
| INFLATION | 2.37% |
| AVG. ASSET ALLOCATION INVESTOR | 2.53% |
| HEDGE FUNDS | 5.43% |
| INTERNATIONAL EQUITIES | 5.68% |
| BONDS | 5.74% |
| GOLD | 5.78% |
| S&P 500 TR | 9.22% |
| OIL | 9.32% |
| PRIVATE INVESTMENTS | 15.06% |

How do you potentially realize better than 2.5 percent on your money? The simple answer is this: the right strategy, one that endowments and institutions such as Yale and others employ—a strategy that diversifies your overall

---

5    PerTrac, January 1, 1994–December 31, 2013.

portfolio in both public and private investments, which provides true multiple-asset-class diversification resulting in reduced correlation.

We'll get into the nuts and bolts of this institutional investment strategy in the next chapter, but let's keep a wider focus for the time being. Here's what Kalos Financial's Daniel Wildermuth has to say about this strategy in his book *Wise Money*:

> Success results from strategy, not exceptional skills, access, or experience. The implications to individual investors are tremendous because individuals can copy strategy, and the rapid expansion of investments has provided individuals access to similar types of investments used by endowments.[6]

Let's focus on that last concept. Individual investors now have greater access to endowment-type investments, including non-market-correlated investments in private equity, venture capital, and real estate, than they have in the past.

Formerly, only "accredited investors" were able to invest in private securities at all. The SEC defines an accredited investor as someone with a million dollars in assets, exclusive of their personal residence, or who has earned

6    Daniel Wildermuth, *Wise Money* (New York: McGraw-Hill Education, 2012), 4.

a minimum of $200,000 in each of the last two years—$300,000 for couples filing together. In other words, high-net-worth individuals and families.

A few ultra-high-net-worth individuals were wealthy enough to make traditional institutional-style investments through their "family offices." If you had millions of dollars in loose change, you could pay to play and diversify your portfolio accordingly. Until recently, you needed millions of dollars if you wanted to play with the big boys and take advantage of endowment-style investments.

Then, in 2012, Congress passed the Jumpstart Our Business Startups (JOBS) Act, which was expanded in 2017. The JOBS Act was intended to give more people access to private investments, because private investments can help the economy. Now even non-accredited investors have access to certain private, non-correlated investments.

When you invest in private equity and venture capital, you're often investing in smaller businesses that may currently have relatively modest revenues of, say, $25 million a year or less. When you make these private investments, you create jobs and growth in vital sectors of the economy, such as technology, agriculture, and commercial real estate.

Look at Silicon Valley. At one time, not so long ago, Apple,

Google, Facebook, and Uber were all startups. Now, they're billion-dollar companies.

When Apple and Google were startups, you had to be able to pay to play. You had to be an accredited investor just to put in opening stakes. Ultra-high-net-worth individuals and families had the advantage of being able to stay in the game longer than even most accredited investors.

The landscape has changed dramatically in the last seven years. Private investments in commercial real estate, for example, are now available to non-accredited investors, and accredited investors have access to more private-asset investment opportunities than ever before.

Times have changed. A radically new investment strategy, one that has kept pace with the times so far and, in my opinion, is both needed and now possible.

## THE ALTERNATIVE STRATEGY

Most people have been getting the same investment advice—a traditional 60/40 stocks/bonds portfolio—for the last twenty to forty years, and they're still getting it today. The sad truth is, most likely, that your investment broker's advice is straight out of the Jurassic era.

Why? Most financial advisors are simply not educated in

the institutional-endowment investment model. Most are not educated in, nor do they understand, how to make and reap the benefits of alternative, non-publicly traded investments. A major brokerage firm is probably giving different and better advice to someone who's already one of the "big boys." Both independent brokers and most brokers with large firms know as little about alternative investment strategies as you do. One of the reasons is many major brokerages are not interested in doing due diligence on these offerings, because they are not large enough to be offered throughout their brokerage systems.

The purpose of this book is to change all of that and educate you about a genuinely new and improved investment strategy. As you'll see, in this case "new and improved" isn't merely a marketing ploy but a genuine and newly available alternative to the market-correlated roller-coaster ride.

Alternative investments are the cornerstone of The Household Endowment Model (THEM). And like a cornerstone, alternative investments are one part of the larger whole. Let's return to the overall THEM model set forth in the introduction before delving more deeply into endowment-style investment strategy.

As mentioned, most high-net-worth families contend with the following five primary concerns:

## Five Key Concerns
of the Affluent

**1** **Wealth Preservation**
Protecting Your Wealth

**2** **Wealth Enhancement**
Mitigating Taxes

**3** **Wealth Transfer/Estate Planning**
Taking Care of Heirs

**4** **Wealth Protection/Asset Protection**
No Unjust Loss

**5** **Charitable Giving**

1. Wealth Preservation: Investment consulting to maximize the probability of achieving financial goals. This is where endowment-style investing enters the picture. When speaking before groups of investors, I always ask anyone who wants to lose money to raise their hand. No hands are raised. That's what wealth preservation is all about.

2. Wealth Enhancement: After the family investment portfolio is stabilized, attention shifts to mitigating tax liability while helping ensure the family has the cash flow it needs. When speaking before groups of investors, I ask anyone who wants to pay more money in taxes to raise their hand. Again, no hands are raised. Most families don't want to pay more taxes than legally necessary. Paying less in taxes means that they have more to invest for themselves. Always remember that it's not what you make that counts; it's what you keep.

3. Wealth Transfer and Estate Planning: The smoothest, most tax-efficient way to pass on assets to loved ones. You would like to choose where your assets are going to go on your demise rather than have courts rule where they should go or have your family members arguing about who gets what. That's why it's so important to put everything down in black and white in an estate-planning document.

4. Wealth Protection/Asset Protection: Protecting accumulated wealth from creditors, litigants, potential lawsuits, and catastrophic loss.

5. Charitable Giving: Fulfilling charitable goals in the ways most beneficial to their families and the causes they care about.

The chapters that follow in part 1 will focus on the first pillar, "Wealth Preservation," which involves investment counseling meant to maximize the possibility of you achieving your and your family's financial goals. The bad news is that your dinosaur-era investment strategy may not achieve this. The good news is that THEM is an alternative in every sense of the word. *This is not to say that there is no risk in this strategy.* The goal is to mitigate the risk.

If you don't want to relive 2008—and who does?—you need a new strategy. And you're about to learn about such new strategies and their potential.

# CHAPTER 2

# INSTITUTIONAL INVESTING: THE YALE ENDOWMENT MODEL

To preserve and build your wealth and to get a potentially better return on your investments, you need to be able to play with the proverbial "big boys." Institutional investors traditionally get the best returns because they have the most money and access to work with. The big news, which most investors and even most investment counselors haven't yet caught on to, is that it's now possible for any accredited, and even unaccredited, investor to participate in endowment-style investments.

## A CHANGE FOR THE (MUCH) BETTER

The state-of-the-art institutional investment strategy is the Yale Endowment Model, which has been adopted by other major institutional investment funds. Eager adopters include such academic powerhouses as Harvard, Stanford, Princeton, and Dartmouth and major pension plans like CalSTRS, the California-state teacher-retirement fund, and ERS, the Texas State Employee Retirement System.

The driving force behind the Yale model is its brilliant chief investment officer, David Swensen, who began running the fund in 1985 and has completely transformed it since. His approach is highly researched and based on the work of Nobel economics laureates James Tobin and Harry Markowitz, among many others.

Before getting into the practice and theory behind the Yale Endowment Model, let's look at results. In investment, the bottom line rules, and Yale's bottom line is calculated to blow away anyone who looks into it for the first time. For a snapshot, take a look at this graph comparing returns from the Yale model to the traditional 60/40 investment model in the period from 1999 to 2018:[7]

---

7    *The Yale Endowment*, reports for years 1999–2018; S&P 500; Barclays Bond Index.

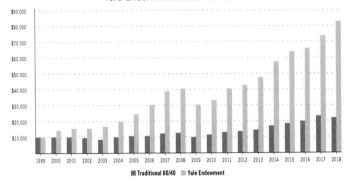

Yale Endowment Model vs. 60/40

Traditional 60/40    Yale Endowment

Wow! Why would you ever have a Jurassic-era 60/40 port-folio when the endowment model might give you such a potentially improved return on investment (ROI)? Individual investors may not earn as much as Yale does, given the size of its endowment and its liquidity needs, but they would have possibly earned more than they could have by going the traditional route during this time period.[8]

How are these spectacular results achieved? Fortunately, you don't need to delve into the academic work of Nobel economics laureates to understand the nuts-and-bolts investment practices that have brought about such spectacular results.

In 1985, when David Swensen started managing the Yale Endowment, its assets were invested fairly conventionally: almost 65 percent in domestic US stocks, which was very close to the standard 60/40 model. That started

---

8    60 percent S&P 500; 40 percent Barclays Credit Index.

changing radically in the early '90s, as the following graph shows:[9]

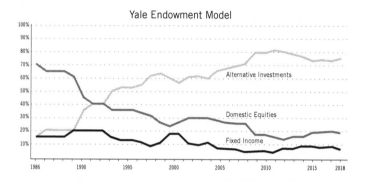

Making alternative rather than conventional investments is the heart of the strategy that has paid off so brilliantly.

As you can see, Swensen started making alternative investments as soon as he began running the fund in 1985. It took a while to make the switch, but alternatives overtook conventional investments in US market-traded stocks in the mid-'90s.

David Swensen has exponentially increased the value of Yale's institutional portfolio by reducing conventional US equity investments from 65 to 20 percent and, conversely, by increasing investments in alternative investments from 20 to 70 percent.

---

9    *The Yale Endowment*, reports for years 1986-2018.

## ALTERNATIVE INVESTMENTS: THE BASICS

Digging deeper, the question becomes this: what's an alternative investment? Perhaps more to the point, what "alternative" asset classes does Yale invest in? The following chart gives a general idea:[10]

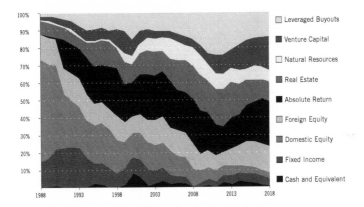

"Leveraged buyouts," "venture capital," "natural resources," "real estate," and "absolute return" are all alternative and, in many cases, private investments. "Private" means they are not traded through public markets and are therefore not correlated to the public-market roller coaster. "Alternative" means that they are not conventional investment vehicles but simply alternatives to conventional publicly traded investments.

Most mutual funds claim asset diversification as one of their strengths. However, such diversification is generally restricted to publicly traded financial instruments, mean-

10  http://investments.yale.edu/.

ing the portfolio as a whole is still highly correlated to public markets. What Swensen and the Yale Endowment Fund have done is *real* diversification, moving beyond public markets into the private sphere. When Swensen started implementing this plan, such a strategy was only available to funds the size of the Yale Endowment and the ultra-wealthy. No longer!

A primary reason for the Yale Endowment's stunning success may be the so-called illiquidity premium. For the moment, suffice it to say that investing in privately traded, illiquid assets such as real estate means that you can't divest yourself of them at a moment's notice. This prevents emotionally driven bad investment decisions and may contribute to greater overall yields. The "illiquidity premium" will be discussed in greater detail in the next chapter.

There's another key component to the Yale Endowment strategy that needs to be underlined. As the Yale Investments Office itself put it in a 2017 white paper, "We work to establish an appropriate risk-adjusted asset allocation and seek out long-term partnerships across the globe with managers who provide deep analytical insights and improve the operations of public and private businesses."

To paraphrase and emphasize the key point here, Yale makes long-term investments with managers whom they believe to be "best-of-breed" in specific asset classes. Swensen, brilliant as he is, can't keep track of what's going on at a granular level in each of the asset classes Yale invests in, and neither can his staff. Nobody can, which is why specialist experts are needed. If you're going to make alternative, private investments, you need to assemble a team of experienced investment managers, each of whom specializes in a certain asset class.

As an example, "natural resources" include oil and gas on the one hand and timber on the other. If you are going to invest in both types of natural resources, you need to form two partnerships, one each with an expert investor in each category. That's what Yale does. Much more on this, and what it means to individual investors, below.

David Swensen started a revolution that many other, duly impressed, institutional investors have joined. He created a roadmap that now not only institutional investors but investment counselors whose clients are mainly individual investors and families can follow. That's an exciting story that as yet very few investors and investment counselors have heard.

What this means is that, as an individual investor, you may now play with the big boys in their sandbox. Before I show you how, another question needs to be answered:

how and why do alternative, private investments potentially outperform public, market-correlated ones?

# CHAPTER 3

# ALTERNATIVE INVESTMENTS: DIGGING DEEPER

"Alternative investments" has a nice ring to it, but what does it really mean? To begin with, you now know that these are generally private investments rather than ones made in publicly traded markets. (We'll get into a more precise definition a little later.) Therefore, they are not correlated with public markets' ups and downs. What is it about alternative investments that may make them such a great addition to the conventional stock/bond portfolio?

For a first cut at an answer, let's go straight to the source. Here's what the Yale Investment Office has to say:

> [Yale's] heavy allocation to non-traditional asset classes

stems from their return potential and diversifying power...
Alternative assets, by their very nature, tend to be less
efficiently priced than traditional marketable securities,
providing an opportunity to exploit market inefficiencies
through active management. The Endowment's long-time
horizon is well suited to exploiting illiquid, less efficient
markets, such as venture capital, leveraged buyouts, oil
and gas, timber, and real estate.[11]

## THE ILLIQUIDITY PREMIUM

"Illiquidity" and "market inefficiencies" sound like neg-
atives rather than positives. Counterintuitively, when it
comes to making the greatest return on your investment,
the opposite can turn out to be the case.

Remember the account of the emotional, knee-jerk reac-
tion to the crash of 2008 in chapter 1? Investors sold when
the market was at its lowest, hoping to "save" what was
left. The same was true of many large financial institutions and mutual funds. Even when the people at the
helm knew better—and let's hope at least some of them
did—they were forced to liquidate holdings at the worst
possible time, because, in many cases, their charters
forced them to.

By the time the market started turning around in late

---

11  Yale Investments Office, "Yale Investment Policy," 2017.

2009, it was too late to recoup losses. The money had already gone down the drain, in large part because of so-called market efficiencies. An "efficient market" is one that rapidly reflects and adjusts to changing facts on the ground. In general, in an efficient market, securities are neither under- nor overvalued. They are priced in a way that reflects all relevant, available information.

Market efficiency and liquidity go hand-in-hand. In an efficient market, you can easily buy low and sell high. The problem is that it's just as easy to buy high and sell low. In fact, it's all too simple to push the panic button when the market's roller coaster accelerates from a peak down into a valley.

Illiquidity and inefficient markets can potentially save some investors from themselves. To take a simple example: an investment in privately held commercial real estate requires a long-term commitment of capital, often five years or more. If you think you need your money back in two years, you're basically out of luck—which turns out to be lucky in some cases. Therefore, when looking at these types of investments, your advisor needs to know your liquidity needs and plan accordingly when constructing your portfolio.

To put this in more formal financial terms, the potentially higher returns attributed to alternative, in contrast to conventional, investments may be attributed to the "illiquidity premium." Although several factors are at play, the more liquid an investment is, typically the less risk is involved and the lower the return. The standard risk/reward equation, with which you may be familiar, comes into play: the higher the risk, the higher the reward for success, because the chance of failure is comparably high. Much has been written about the illiquidity premium, and the subject can be extensively researched.

As an example of what has been written on the subject, in September 2014, the Blackstone Group, a New York-based private equity, alternative-asset management and financial services firm, published a paper titled "Patient Capital, Private Opportunity: The Benefits and Challenges of Illiquid Alternatives."[12] Its topic is the "illiquid opportunity and illiquid advantage" of "patient capital," meaning capital invested for the longer rather than shorter term. The paper states, "The lack of a public market for these assets and their resulting illiquidity is the primary source of both the benefits and challenges they present."

What does this mean? Again, in an efficient public market, information is available in real time and assets can be

---

12    http://www.heritagegroup.ca/sites/default/files/users/db/PDFs/Patient%20Capital%20-%20
Private%20Opportunity.pdf.

traded immediately. This creates a relatively uniform market in which most investors have equal chances of profit and loss. Public markets are transparent because it is illegal to trade on insider information. This market transparency delivers returns that are "symmetric"— more or less the same—for most investors.

Private markets and private investments operate with an entirely different set of rules. Private companies are not required to disclose corporate information to the public. So-called insider trading is not illegal but rather the name of the game. As a result, investors in these companies have greater or "asymmetric" access to information about company management, company financials, sales pipelines, and strategies.

In short, market inefficiencies can give patient investors, those willing and with the financial ability to wait long enough to make illiquid investments, advantages and opportunities over investors in publicly traded, highly liquid markets. The Yale Endowment Fund, the Blackstone Group, and The Household Endowment Model (THEM) all understand and leverage these advantages for the benefit of their clients.

Russ Koesterich, chief investment strategist at BlackRock, a prominent investment management firm, thinks there are plenty of reasons to favor illiquidity:

The general need and preference for liquidity drives up the prices of liquid alternatives, allowing longer-term investors (like large institutions) to collect an "illiquidity premium"— the flipside of which is the "liquidity penalty" suffered by liquid alternatives. Because they are not driven by daily price changes, illiquid investments can deliver more return and downside protection over the mid- to long-term, too. Illiquid investments are perhaps especially appropriate for well-capitalized investors who do not require continuous ready access to their assets. Some endowments increasingly prefer private equity holdings to publicly traded equity shares.[13]

With illiquid investments, Koesterich concludes, investors still tend to get paid for locking up their money for a specific period.

## DIFFERENT ALTERNATIVES

Once you move beyond the prehistoric 60/40 stock/bond investment portfolio, possibilities rapidly expand and increase. Take a look at the following graph:

---

13   https://equityinstitutional.com/EquityInstitutional/media/Documents/Whitepapers/
     Marketing/liquid-illiquid-alternatives.pdf.

# A Portfolio of Possibilities

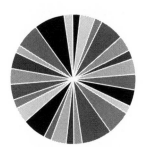

CDs and Money Markets
Tactical Currency Manager
Tax Credit Program
Bank Structured Notes
Life Settlement Notes
Tactical Income
Fixed Income & Bonds
Fixed Indexed Annuity
**Venture Capital**
**Private Equity Real Estate**
Business Development Co.
**Real Estate Development**
**Oil and Gas Programs**

**Private Equities/IPOs**
**Private Credit**
Strategic Modern Portfolio
US Sector Rotation Model
International Country Rotation
**Conservation Easement**
SMA Tactical Constrained Strategies
SMA Tactical Unconstrained Strategies
Global Macro Tactical
**Value Add Real Estate**
Managed Futures
Commodities Long Strategy
Absolute Return Long/Short

The above is a sample of the many different asset classes investors may have available. (Note that alternative-investment classes are listed in boldface.) This pie has thirty-three slices, which is somewhat overwhelming. The real question, however, is why your investment advisor may only be serving up two or three of them. The answer is they probably don't even know about, or know enough about, the other options.

Some clarification is needed at this point. No portfolio, institutional or individual, should consist entirely of private alternative investments. Even David Swensen didn't divest the Yale Endowment of all its publicly traded stocks or even bonds.

Another fine-print point of clarification: Alternative investments are non-correlated to public markets, but some are still publicly, as opposed to privately, traded. A mutual fund, for instance, could be designed so that its various investments do not move in sync. Commodity futures are publicly traded but not correlated to market movements. Hedge funds and similar financial instruments, such as so-called interval funds, are relatively liquid but don't move in lockstep with the stock market.

These non-correlated investments are alternatives to the usual 60/40 model, but, being publicly traded, they may not offer an illiquidity premium. However, since they are publicly traded, they are relatively liquid, and the knee-jerk response might well be to sell them during a market decline or meltdown.

Because of this "leakage" problem, private offerings are a better focus for alternative investment. This means you can't just wake up one morning, hear that the Dow Jones is down a thousand points, and rush to the phone or computer to sell your private investments like you can your publicly traded ones. This book won't be focusing on publicly traded alternative investments for this very reason, which means we don't need to get into details about hedge or interval funds and their "cousins."

A number of the pie's thirty-three pieces are alternative, non-correlated private investments with an illiquidity advantage. Two of the most important categories here are venture capital and private equity. We'll look at these in greater depth in the next chapter, which will also deal with what Blackstone calls the "challenges," as well as benefits, of illiquid investments.

Rather than try to cover every category of illiquid, alternative investment here, let's look more closely at two other important categories: real estate and natural resources.

## REAL ESTATE

Owning their own homes is the most common, and biggest, investment most people make. A house is a relatively illiquid investment, although of course people buy and sell homes all the time. However, when the residential real estate market becomes too liquid, there's generally trouble ahead, and that's just what happened when the housing bubble burst in the run-up to 2008.

The focus here will not be on owning your own home or buying and flipping single-family residences but on larger-scale commercial and multifamily residential investments. This form of alternative investment is in equity rather than a specific asset like the house across the street.

Real estate investments have shown very low correlation with publicly traded markets over time. They also offer two potential benefits: cash flow and price appreciation. Despite such incidents as the bursting of the housing bubble, real estate investments overall show a steady stream of returns over many investment cycles in certain sectors. To illustrate these general principles, let's look at four specific, concrete examples, three in commercial and one in residential real estate.

One of our institutional investment relationships is with a real estate investment firm with offices throughout the South whose focus is industrial warehouses. It locates assets to invest in and uses the money raised from investors to grow its commercial real estate portfolio. It pays you both for the use of your money along the way, through dividends from cash flow, and by sharing the equity growth that has been created when the fund closes out.

Let's say the company creates a portfolio of a hundred properties over two years that you invest in. During that time, it leased the warehouses to Amazon, FedEx, UPS, and similar companies. Along the way, the fund pays you an income dividend. You share in the operating income that's generated from the leases on each of those buildings.

At the end of five years or so, your equity payday arrives. At that time, the company sells the hundred-building portfolio it's built to a major institution, such as an insurance company, a corporate pension fund, a private-sector retirement plan, or a publicly traded real estate investment trust (REIT).

As an example, one such big institutional player might be CalSTRS, the California Teachers Retirement System, which is probably the largest pension fund in the country. CalSTRS has hundreds of billions of dollars in its fund.[14] It doesn't have the time to look for "small" investments in the $5 million, $10 million, or $20 million range. It isn't interested. It's looking to invest hundreds of millions of dollars at a time.

Institutions like CalSTRS rely on companies like this real estate investment firm to do the work of creating aggregated portfolios. The company's specialty is buying warehouse buildings in the $5-million-to-$25-million range, which it is potentially able to acquire for less than market value because of its expertise and relationships. Once it buys a hundred such buildings, it has a portfolio worth half a billion dollars.

CalSTRS is now interested. It thanks the company for creating the portfolio and buys it more for the income it will produce than for upside growth. That income will be used to pay its members' pensions. When the portfolio is sold, the company pays an equity premium to its investors, who are now that much wealthier.

Another such company is a real estate investment trust (known in the trade as a "REIT") whose MO bears both

---

14  https://www.calstrs.com/sites/main/files/file-attachments/fastfacts_2018.pdf.

similarities to and differences from the previous example. The difference is its focus on Main Street retail real estate rather than industrial warehouses, but the process is much the same. It launches investment funds meant to purchase and accumulate sites on the Main Street corners in places where companies like Walgreens, CVS, and Bank of America want to set up business. Their goal is to be on the corners of high-traffic intersections in single free-standing building locations rather than in malls or strip centers.

Walgreens may say, for instance, "We want so many locations in these types of areas in these cities." The company sets up an investment fund—a REIT—to find and buy the land and build new or acquire existing buildings. It then signs long-term leases, typically for twenty years or more, with Walgreens, by way of example. This is done over and over again until the fund has created a portfolio of, say, 300 retail commercial real estate properties. Then, like the company in the previous example, it will sell the portfolio as a whole to an institutional investor or a large public REIT, with its investors all sharing in the equity profits. Along the way, while building this portfolio, it will pay investors a dividend from operating income.

A third real estate alternative-investments approach is a debt fund consisting of private debt backed by real estate assets. The fund raises, say, $30 million to $50 million and will pay you, by way of example, 7 to 9 percent annually for the use of the money you invest.

The company in this example buys and develops centers with multiple retail tenants. These are not strip malls or enclosed malls but the large multiuse retail centers where you might find both a T.J. Maxx and a Whole Foods.

The company actually borrows money from its investors and then goes out to buy land and develop or acquire these retail sites, signing long-term leases with tenants. The owner of the company in this example puts a personal guarantee on every transaction. The actual builders or developers of the commercial real estate center also put in their capital or equity. Under these conditions, the entire equity invested would have to disappear before there would be any risk to your debt-fund investment.

The difference between this approach and that of the REIT in the last example is that the company issuing the debt opportunity isn't as concerned if the value of the property goes up or down, because it's not going to sell the property to an institution like CalSTRS, hoping to make money. All it's doing is borrowing money to develop or acquire the property.

As an investor, you will basically receive an income stream. For example, the debt fund gets to use your money for three years, generates an income stream for that time, and gives you back the money you've invested at the end of the period. There's no equity involved. As an investor, you're now looking to make income in the short term rather than a profit in the long term.

There are many different debt funds, but they all look about the same. They all borrow capital to grow an asset. As an investor, you're not locked into equity, so you don't take any equity risk. Your entire involvement and risk are on the debt side, so the whole fund would literally have to have a significant decrease in equity before there would be risk of impacting your income stream or the principal you originally invested.

In a fourth and final example, we'll move from commercial to residential real estate. Again, this doesn't mean buying and flipping single-family residences or even apartment buildings. It means buying and selling housing subdivisions.

The company in this example is a large home builder in North Texas. Again, a real estate-backed debt fund is established to raise the capital to buy land and develop a subdivision. The homes and land are used as collateral to secure the funds borrowed from investors. Then the houses are sold, completing a cycle that typically occurs once or twice a year. The company generally makes a profit on each house sold and pays investors 9 percent annually for the use of their money.

Let me remind you that, as with any investment, these strategies do not offer any guarantees as to the return of principal or payment of the stated income or dividends. However, proper due diligence should demonstrate their overall performance and may make them opportunities well worth considering for qualified investors.

## NATURAL RESOURCES

Natural resources offer many opportunities for often highly profitable alternative investments. Energy in particular is a great way of getting into non-correlated investments and alternative investment strategies. One of the main advantages is that, because of the way the tax code is written, there are valuable tax benefits for investing in energy.

Everybody has heard of oil wildcatters who take $100,000 to dig a well in Texas that hits a gusher and generates millions or billions of dollars in revenue. The other side of the coin is that the wildcatter could put $100,000 into digging what turns out to be a dry well without a drop of oil in it.

The government wants more investment in energy, and

natural gas is a particular focus these days. Ten years ago, the United States was a net importer of natural gas. Now, we will soon be the largest exporter of natural gas in the world, if we aren't already. Our natural gas resources equal and exceed Saudi Arabia's oil reserves. Natural gas is used to make fertilizer and plastics and to generate electricity, and it is being increasingly used as a vehicle fuel. Demand is growing significantly.

One of our energy-development companies is a Pittsburgh-based, multi-billion-dollar family office that has been in business for seventy-five years. At launch, it was primarily involved in coal mining but now deals with natural gas.

During the coal-mining days, the company acquired land all over the region—150,000 acres—which is part of what geologists call the Marcellus Shale Formation. This the largest natural gas field in the United States and the second-largest in the world. You could basically go stick a long straw down into the ground in the Marcellus Formation and find natural gas, so to speak. I think you get the point.

Technology advances mean that wells can now be drilled horizontally as well as vertically. Once you get to a certain depth you can hang a left or a right and continue on for several miles, all of which significantly increases the opportunity for capturing more gas.

Although family-run, the firm has an investment fund that may raise $50 million or more in a year and then invest its own money alongside investors'. Because of energy tax-law advantages, under current law investors can write off approximately 80 percent of their investment in the first year and an additional 10 percent in the second year. Within twelve months, investors might see an income of 2 to 3 percent on their investment monthly, depending on the current price of natural gas. This initiates an income stream that will eventually decrease because of natural-gas depletion but could last for another twenty-five to fifty years, depending on the type of drilling and technology used.

Since you don't get a dividend from money you send to the IRS, you might want to consider investing in such an energy company instead. Under current tax law, you'll get an approximately 80 percent tax write-off the first year, 10 percent in the second year, and potentially an annual dividend check, which also allows for a 15 percent discount on the distributed taxable income.

Of course, any alternative investment, such as those in natural resources, require your accountant's or CPA's input to determine if they will be effective in the context of your personal financial and tax situation. We always recommend seeking your tax and legal specialists' professional opinions and do not give such advice ourselves.

However, we are always happy to refer your tax and legal experts to ours. And of course, there is no guarantee of success or results in these types of investments.

That's a rapid tour of some sample alternative investments. Now let's look in greater depth at two of the most popular private, non-correlated alternative investments: venture capital and private equity.

# CHAPTER 4

# VENTURE CAPITAL AND PRIVATE EQUITY

Before diving in, let's back up a bit. Alternative investments provide alternatives to the 60/40 portfolio. This does *not* mean that your portfolio should consist entirely of alternative and specifically private, non-correlated, illiquid investments. It *does* mean, however, that—based on your risk profile, time horizon, and liquidity needs— your portfolio should include private investments and not be limited to public ones.

## VENTURE CAPITAL

Get ready for several surprises. For most individual investors, the first surprise is that, historically, venture capital—investing in startup or early-stage entrepreneurial enterprises—has been one of the most profitable long-term investment vehicles.[15] Given what we know about the illiquidity premium, it should come as no surprise that venture capital is also the most illiquid—or is that the "least liquid"?—investment you can make.

Another way of thinking about a properly diversified portfolio for qualified investors is that some of your investments should be in a "liquid" bucket and some in an "illiquid" bucket. David Swensen's innovation at the Yale Endowment Fund was his ever-greater emphasis on illiquid investments that have historically been more profitable in the long run.[16]

Another core tenet of the Yale Endowment philosophy is employing outside managers who are perceived as experts in their fields to make and oversee investments in the asset classes in which they have expertise. One of the experts we consult with regularly is venture capital funds manager Carter Williams, who helped launch Boeing Ventures before starting his own fund. He and his team have broad expertise in early-stage technology and co-invest with other leading venture firms. While most venture funds are reserved for the ultra-wealthy, his firm is structured to work with more modest THEM

---

15  https://www.cambridgeassociates.com/private-investment-benchmarks/.

16  http://investments.yale.edu/reports.

allocations. Much of the following information on venture capital comes from interviews done with Carter.

## UPSIDE AND PROVISOS

The following chart starkly spells out the advantages of venture-capital investment:[17]

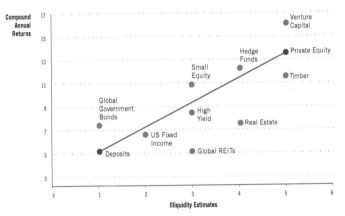

Investment Returns Generally Increase with Degree of Illiquidity

Venture capital's position in the upper right-hand corner of this graph indicates that it both provides the highest compound annual returns and is the most illiquid asset class for the time period shown. The data reflects that compounded annual returns are correlated with illiquid-

---

17  From "Expected Returns," by Antti Illmanen, 2011. Scatterplotting average asset returns 1990-2009 on (subjective) illiquidity estimates. Sources: Bloomberg, MSCI Barra, Ken French's website, Citigroup, Barclays Capital, JP Morgan, Bank of America Merrill Lynch, S&P GSCI, MIT-CRE, FTSE, Global Property Research, UBS, NCREIF, Hedge Fund Research, Cambridge Associates.

ity. Venture capital and private equity, which we'll look at a bit later and whose position in the chart is second only to venture capital, tend to offer increased returns over more liquid investments, but they may come with additional risk.

Venture capital invests in startup, early-stage, and emerging companies. While investing in new opportunities may be one of the world's oldest investment approaches, it was first institutionalized when Georges Doriot founded American Research and Development (ARD) in 1946.[18]

Doriot famously said, "Someone, somewhere, is making a product that will make your product obsolete." Investors hire venture capitalists to find entrepreneurs with the resourcefulness to create new products that make existing products obsolete. The first venture-capital home run was ARD's $70,000 investment in Digital Equipment Corporation, which grew to $400 million by the time the holding was liquidated.

The Kauffman Foundation's analysis of over 3,000 early-stage venture-capital investments showed that they generated a 27 percent rate of return over three and a half years.[19]

---

18  https://apinstitutional.invesco.com/dam/jcr:1f35880c-bdf9-42ea-8afe-ab69b85bc7a4/
The%20Case%20for%20Venture%20Capital.pdf.

19  https://papers.ssrn.com/sol3/papers.cfm?abstract_id=1028592.

Of course, when investing, the only guarantee is that there are no iron-clad guarantees. Properly diversified venture-capital assets have outperformed all other asset classes in the long term, with emphasis on "long term" and "properly diversified." But no asset class is entirely immune to poor economic conditions and business cycles, or to the mistakes of poor managers.

However, because venture capital is focused on private investment in disruptive products and fundamental productivity enhancements, venture returns are largely shielded from direct market volatility and monetary policy shifts such as changes in interest rates. Put another way, if you make a pill to cure a disease, the market will see its value, regardless of the highs and lows of the Dow Jones.

## THE ENTREPRENEURIAL ADVANTAGE

Historically, the single greatest producer of wealth has been investment in private companies and the entrepreneurs who lead them. As Carter Williams puts it, "American entrepreneurs use 'creative destruction' to transform economic structures, advance technologies, and raise living standards globally, generating tremendous profits along the way."[20]

---

20 https://www.chicagofed.org/-/media/publications/chicago-fed-letter/2014/cflseptember2014-326-pdf.pdf.

Amazon, Google, Facebook, Airbnb, and Uber were all startups at one point. Indeed, every big company was once small—usually very small, generally with one or two people in a room or the proverbial garage with an idea and a phone. Growing small startups into big companies is never easy. You start with one or two employees and then expand to five, ten, twenty, and more. In fact, entrepreneurs are among the economy's biggest job-creators.[21]

While the Amazons and Apples of the world were all originally funded by venture capital, venture-capital funds have also invested in many startups that failed. In fact, they have invested in more failures than successes.[22] Only 25 percent of investments return investors' capital,[23] with yet fewer portfolio companies returning the bulk of portfolio return.

Because individual startups are far more likely to fail than to succeed, venture-capital investments seem risky. Why, then, as the following chart shows, does venture capital as an asset class consistently outperform other asset classes?

21  https://www.mitpressjournals.org/doi/pdf/10.1162/REST_a_00288.

22  http://www.industryventures.com/2017/02/07/the-venture-capital-risk-and-return-matrix/.

23  https://www.wsj.com/articles/SB10000872396390443720204578004980476429190.

## US Venture Capital

*Fund Index Summary: Horizon Pooled Return*

AS OF SEPTEMBER 30, 2018

| INDEX | 5-YEAR | 10-YEAR | 15-YEAR | 20-YEAR | 25-YEAR |
|---|---|---|---|---|---|
| Cambridge Associates LLC US Venture Capital Index | 15.59 | 11.06 | 10.69 | 24.75 | 29.83 |
| US Venture Capital–Early Stage Index | 16.99 | 11.40 | 10.49 | 97.06 | 43.64 |
| US Venture Capital–Late and Expansion Stage Index | 12.03 | 11.71 | 11.53 | 9.50 | 11.50 |
| US Venture Capital–Multi-Stage Index | 14.50 | 10.30 | 10.78 | 9.76 | 13.95 |
| Bloomberg Barclays Capital Government/Credit Bond Index | 2.23 | 3.95 | 3.75 | 4.48 | 5.02 |
| Dow Jones Industrial Average Index | 14.57 | 12.22 | 9.97 | 8.79 | 10.91 |
| Dow Jones US Small Cap Index | 10.53 | 11.69 | 10.62 | 10.85 | 10.41 |
| Dow Jones US Top Cap Index | 13.79 | 12.10 | 9.92 | 7.65 | 9.78 |
| Nasdaq Composite Index | 16.36 | 14.42 | 10.55 | 8.10 | 9.88 |
| Russell 1000 Index | 13.67 | 12.09 | 9.85 | 7.70 | 9.87 |
| Russell 2000 Index | 11.07 | 11.11 | 10.12 | 9.45 | 9.38 |
| S&P 500 Index | 13.95 | 11.97 | 9.65 | 7.42 | 9.81 |
| Wilshire 5000 Total Market Index | 13.63 | 12.02 | 9.97 | 7.92 | 9.78 |

Carter Williams's intriguing answer to that question is "illiquidity and surprise!"

## THE BENEFITS AND PERILS OF LIQUIDITY

Let's start with illiquidity, whose advantages we've already discussed, and apply it to venture capital. Much of what is said here will also apply to private-equity investments.

Let's say your grandparents or parents left you their original investment in Pfizer, first made when its predecessor, American Home Products, went public in 1926 and untouched since. If they invested $1,000 at the time, it would be worth about $867,716.33 today. Lucky you!

However, Cambridge Associate research reports a historic venture-capital return rate for the last twenty-five years of 28.2 percent per year.[24] If you had invested your Pfizer money in 1926 at a 28.2 percent annual return rate, your $1,000 would have turned into $10,804,043,945,161.70 today.

The irony is that while Pfizer was liquid the entire time, nostalgia for your grandparents' original investment made their investment essentially illiquid, without the benefits of an illiquidity premium. Are you at risk because you've invested your illiquidity premium money in nostalgia?

New ventures have ups and downs, but, because the investment is private, the entrepreneur, rather than worrying about an enterprise's quarterly stock price, stays focused on understanding customers and building the company. And because the company is illiquid, the entrepreneur is compelled to discount their stock price when venture capitalists make their initial investment.

Most investors have a strong tendency to put liquidity first. "What if I need cash in six months, twelve months, or two years?" What if, indeed! As Michael Milken has said, "Liquidity is an illusion...It's always there when you

---

24   https://www.cambridgeassociates.com/press-releases/
      us-venture-capital-returns-strengthened-in-third-quarter-2017/.

don't need it, and rarely there when you do."[25] That's why some investors, based on their risk profile, may want to put some of their investments in the liquid bucket—but not all.

The real point is that most investors don't properly calculate how much liquidity they need. Think about how much you would need to live if things were tight, and think about all your public and liquid investments. Then think back to past market downturns. Are there public securities you never sold during those periods because the market was so low? Did you figure out a way to muddle through? The value in those unsold public securities represents your real tolerance for illiquidity. You made an illiquid investment without realizing it, but when you bought that security, you paid a premium up front for its liquidity.

In contrast, a venture capitalist is an expert at negotiating for lower up-front prices based on illiquidity. The entrepreneur needs to raise capital and offers a business plan showing future value. The venture capitalist listens to the entrepreneur's story and responds, "I love your business model, but it will take you eight years to realize its full value. I will invest, but you need to lower the stock price to protect me and my investors from the illiquidity risk."

25  https://www.independent.co.uk/news/business/comment/the-illusion-of-liquidity-is-a-trap-for-investors-in-troubled-markets-10516208.html.

## RISK AND THE ROUNDS

But aren't startups risky ventures almost by definition? Didn't we just say that far more startups fail than succeed? Why should you invest your hard-earned cash in companies that are bound to fail? If there's so much risk involved, why does The Household Endowment Model include venture capital as a critical strategy in its overall investment approach, even if, as in many cases, it's only a small percentage of the overall portfolio?

Venture capital is extraordinarily risky if you don't do due diligence or diversify correctly. What best-of-breed venture capitalists do to mitigate risk is to look at upward of a thousand companies to find reasons not to invest.

This is due diligence with a vengeance, which is absolutely necessary if you're going to invest in startups and early-stage companies. You need to know a lot about the company, the idea, and the people you are investing in. Venture capitalists look at thousands of companies and invest in only a few—those that will have a big impact if they succeed, led by entrepreneurs who, at times when the rest of us would run away, only work harder.

Entrepreneurship is such an important topic these days that most people know there are usually several rounds of investment in new, growing companies. The first round is generally called "seed" funding, with a second and third round to follow as the company requires more capital.

As one round succeeds another, you continue to pay close attention. Most of the companies that you've made a seed or first-round investment in will fall by the wayside. A few will keep charging forward, and you put more of your second- and third-round chips on these.

Why not just wait until the second or third round to invest in later-stage startups that are more likely to succeed? Because, by investing in a startup's seed or first round, you also buy a greater opportunity to invest in the subsequent rounds of companies that thrive.

An analogy Carter Williams likes to use is World Series tickets, saying, "If you buy a season ticket to your city's big-league baseball team's games, you will get the opportunity to buy the team's World Series tickets at face value." It's likely that your team won't make it to the World Series, but if it does, you're guaranteed a reasonably priced seat.

Season-ticket holders have first dibs on World Series games. Likewise, seed-round investors have first dibs on investing in later rounds of companies that look like they're really going to take off. This creates "optionality"—the right but not the obligation to invest.

## THE ELEMENT OF SURPRISE!

Having looked at illiquidity and risk, let's move on to the factor of "surprise." Simply put, a good venture capitalist discovers opportunities that surprise conventional wisdom.

To start thinking like a venture capitalist, ask yourself this: what if you'd had the option to invest in Apple just before the iPhone was announced? Of course, Apple had gone public long before. If you'd bought Apple stock on receiving information, well before the market, about a new product that would transform the world, you'd be breaking insider-trading laws.

Now let's apply this example to the world of non-publicly traded startups. Many people would have done many things differently if they'd known then what they know now. While venture capitalists don't have crystal balls, they do know what others don't. Public companies have analysts who write reports. Private companies don't. The venture capitalist is both early-stage companies' key investor and key analyst. And since venture capitalists invest in technologies long before they go public, they have special knowledge about what's happening well before the public markets do.

When you invest in a startup or other private company, you have greater access to information about the products and services the company is planning to launch and the people on the management team. This knowledge leads to asymmetry between insiders, such as yourself, and outsiders.

To return to our example: if you had known about the iPhone ahead of time, you could have invested in Pandora or the gaming company Zynga, understanding that once Apple's new product hit the stores, a lot of new content would be needed.

None of this is magical. Most of it is really down-to-earth. Data from the Kauffman Foundation, which has done extensive research on entrepreneurship, indicates that what matters most to a venture capital fund is diversification, and what matters most to the startups it invests in is a really strong management team.[26]

What is a surprise to everybody else is, in fact, not a surprise to the venture capitalist. It's routine. Venture capitalists spend their time gleefully using knowledge and "the element of surprise" in private markets. Their information and knowledge about the companies they invest in is so deep that they almost have an unfair advantage.

---

26  https://papers.ssrn.com/sol3/papers.cfm?abstract_id=1028592.

## BEYOND HIGH-TECH UNICORNS

Unicorns used to be lovely mythical beasts in fairy tales or depicted on tapestries. Since the advent of Silicon Valley, they've become the less mythical but still very rare high-tech startups that turn into billion-dollar companies.

Venture capital isn't just about high-tech unicorns, however. In fact, it isn't just about high tech, although people tend to think it is. There are startups in industries of all kinds—health, agriculture, financial services—and in all areas of the country.

"The venture-capital asset class is always going to be a key part of private investing because of its potentially high overall returns," Carter Williams asserts. A startup doesn't need to be a high-tech unicorn to be a highly profitable venture-capital investment. There are thousands of companies that aren't Facebook but should be considered successful if they're part of a venture portfolio that delivers a 15 or 20 percent return. As the Kauffman Foundation has found, diversification is a critical factor in making venture capital the highest-performing asset class—to many people's surprise.[27]

## PRIVATE EQUITY

Private equity is an asset class consisting of equity and

---

27    https://papers.ssrn.com/sol3/papers.cfm?abstract_id=1028592.

debt investments in companies, infrastructure, real estate, and other assets. Capital invested in this asset class is typically raised from a range of investors through private, rather than public, means.

This alternative asset class has existed in some form for decades. From early-stage healthcare technologies to mature, global businesses, from new office buildings to building toll roads, private equity plays an integral part in the global economy. With $4.5 trillion of capital invested and available to invest across a broad range of industries and strategies, private-equity firms play an important role in the global economy and in investors' portfolios.

Entrepreneurial startups aren't the only private enterprises seeking investment. What are known as "middle-market" companies frequently look for capital as well.

Middle-market companies are generally defined as businesses with annual revenues of between $10 million and $1 billion. Many people don't realize that only about 3 percent of US companies are publicly traded. Middle-market companies, a significant category in the remaining 97 percent, account for one-third of the country's private-sector gross domestic product (GDP) and jobs. KitchenAid and Cicis pizza franchises are examples of well-known, durable, middle-market enterprises in relatively stable industries.

As the following chart shows, revenue growth in the middle market has outpaced that in public markets:[28]

| PAST 12 MO. | NEXT 12 MO. |
|---|---|
| **MIDDLE MARKET** | |
| 1Q'19 | 1Q'19 |
| **8.7%** | **5.4%** |
| 4Q'18 **7.9%**  1Q'18 **8.4%** | 4Q'18 **5.9%**  1Q'18 **5.9%** |

| PAST 12 MO. |
|---|
| **S&P 500** |
| 1Q'19 |
| **3.3%** |
| 4Q'18 **4.7%**  1Q'18 **7.4%** |

Many private middle-market companies are looking to grow but, since the crisis of 2008, are finding it more difficult to get capital from traditional funding sources. In recent years, banks and commercial lenders and finance companies have become increasingly regulated and have also been reducing their global balance sheets. To make

---

28   "National Center for the Middle Market Q3 2017 Middle Market Indicator Report" http://www. middlemarketcenter.org/Media/Documents/MiddleMarketIndicators/2017-Q3/FullReport/ NCMM_MMI_Q3_2017_FINAL_web.pdf.

up the shortfall, middle-market firms are increasingly turning to private-equity investment.

Many of the same conditions and provisos that apply to venture capital also apply here. A private-equity manager must have the expertise and experience to do the due diligence needed to locate best-of-category enterprises seeking investment. Experienced managers will generally attempt to locate middle-market enterprises with a well-established market presence, an aligned and seasoned management team, stable and predictable cash flow, and low public-market correlation. Since private-equity investments are relatively illiquid, the advantages, as well as the risks, of illiquidity again apply.

To simplify somewhat, there are two categories of investment in this asset class: private equity and private debt. Frequently, the two types of investment are combined. Equity investment can provide both short-term dividends and the long-term profit participation and distribution that an ownership position can potentially yield. Private debt lending generates short-term interest income.

Private equity is an asset class with both similarities to and differences from venture capital. One similarity is that venture capital and private equity are both alternative asset classes that most investors couldn't invest in until recently. Let's see how that has changed and how you might benefit.

# CHAPTER 5

# YOUR PERSONAL HOUSEHOLD ENDOWMENT MODEL

We've looked in depth at the Yale Endowment institutional investment model, the benefits and importance of alternative, non-correlated investments, and some of these alternative asset classes, with a particular focus on venture capital. The question is this: How does this apply to *you*? How can *you* and your family benefit from an institutional-style investment portfolio?

You've been introduced to many pieces of this puzzle in earlier chapters. Now it's time to fit them all together. After a brief review of basic principles for context, we'll get into some critical aspects of the model that haven't yet been covered.

## BASIC PRINCIPLES

The fundamental answer to the question of how this applies to you is found in The Household Endowment Model (THEM), which applies institutional endowment investment strategies to households, individuals, and families.

THEM is built on three basic principles:

1. We believe, like the Yale Endowment Model, in using "best-of-breed" outside managers to manage individual and family portfolios, and that these expert external managers should be given considerable autonomy to implement strategies as they see fit.
2. A properly allocated portfolio, unlike the traditional 60/40 model, should consist of correlated and non-correlated private and public asset classes.
3. Where there are inefficient markets and illiquidity, opportunity abounds for the patient investor; in particular, we, like Yale, believe that selecting experienced managers in non-public markets can lead to higher returns overall.

## FROM INSTITUTIONS TO HOUSEHOLDS

The Household Endowment Model applies institutional investment strategies to your personal portfolio while taking into account the smaller portfolios of individuals and families compared to institutional investors. The personal application of institutional strategies was previously available only to ultra-high-net-worth families able to hire full-time financial advisors and attorneys in their own "family offices."

The Yale Endowment Model includes both private, non-correlated and publicly traded, market-correlated asset classes, such as the stocks and bonds that make up the entirety of the 60/40 portfolio. This better-balanced portfolio can help smooth out public-market risk and volatility. This model seeks to give our clients the highest probability of achieving their goals without the market-related volatility.

The Household Endowment Model does not aim to get 100 percent of its returns out of venture capital and other alternative investments. The goal with our endowment-style, multi-asset-class approach is diversification into various asset classes that most advisors don't ever consider. These portfolios are actively managed and personalized for meeting investors' particular goals within specified time frames. We seek to provide long-term returns without experiencing the volatile ups and downs that can sometimes include downside swings of 30 to 50 percent.

All your chips are never placed on a single investment, however substantial and promising it may be. Alternative investments are mixed with conventional ones.

It's worth repeating that up until quite recently, individuals could only make the kind of alternative investments institutions like Yale make, as a matter of course, if they were able to write a check for $1 million to $10 million. That price tag is too steep for all but a very few ultra-high-net-worth households.

This recent, dramatic shift was set in motion by the Jumpstart Our Business Startups (JOBS) Act of 2012, revised in 2017. While we won't get bogged down in the details of this legislation, it's worth spelling out some of its key points:

- "Non-accredited" investors, roughly meaning those with less than a million dollars in assets, excluding primary residence, are now able, with certain restrictions, to participate in private investments. This also means that accredited investors have better access to such investments.
- The scope and size of companies that can raise private investment is considerably broadened. Private invest-

ments can now be made in a much wider range of enterprises, both relatively small and relatively larger than before.

- Some of these enterprises can now actively solicit and advertise for such investments.

In short, the JOBS Act loosened up regulations, enabling more people to make a greater variety of investments. The really good news is that the legislation has achieved what it set out to do. Many more people can now invest in venture capital, private equity, commercial and large-scale real estate development, and similar enterprises, helping grow both the economy and their own bank accounts.

The main new factor is the amount and size of alternative investments. Again, you can now participate in the best institutional-style investments with a stake in the $100,000 or even $50,000, rather than $1 million, range. This makes alternative investments viable for many more households than before.

The companies, relationships, and potential private investments we have previously mentioned are now investing side by side with those with considerably smaller pocketbooks. This new source of funding enables them to grow further without taking on institutional partners, who are usually very demanding, controlling, and even fickle.

The sophisticated investors now able to stake $100,000 rather than $1 million-plus in these ventures don't expect or ask for such control. They're glad to be able to hitch a ride on the coattails of these enterprises.

For most of its recent history, the natural-resources company we work with used its own money to drill its natural-gas wells. Now you can invest and potentially profit alongside them. Commercial and large-scale residential real estate ventures and development, once a closed club, have now been opened up to far many more investors. The Household Endowment Model is built on finding these types of private investments and helping clients access them after an extensive due-diligence process.

## ACTIVE MANAGEMENT AND MANAGERS

The Household Endowment Model involves active and experienced investment management in each and every asset class. How does this differ from more common models, including the conventional 60/40 approach?

First, let's contrast active with passive investing, which is possibly the most popular investment strategy in the last twenty years or so. There are many variations on this theme. Your investment advisor may buy a stock index fund, such as Standard and Poor's, that includes 500 publicly traded stocks and then basically just retain those holdings, riding out market fluctuations. No active management is involved, just a reliance on historical data about market performance. To put it bluntly, buying an index is like buying a robot.

Another strategy is to invest in a variety of different public asset categories, notably including mutual funds. The portfolio is then adjusted or "rebalanced" only occasionally and in small increments. The theory, again, is that markets self-correct over time, and a relatively passive strategy enables a portfolio to benefit from historically upward market trends and gradual, long-term growth. While more activity and oversight are involved here than with robotic index-following, the overall strategy is still fundamentally passive.

On the other end of the spectrum is hyperactive, high-frequency trading. Assets are constantly being bought and sold on the basis of almost microscopic incremental changes, generally with the help of a complex computer algorithm or formula. This controversial approach—which is thought to have contributed to some market meltdowns—has yielded enormous profits in some cases. Without getting into arguments pro and con, let's just say that in order to do high-frequency trading, you've generally got to be part of a major financial institution and capable of the difficult and highly abstract mathematics and computer programming involved.

THEM has a different, much more down-to-earth definition of active management. Alternative investments in venture capital, private equity, commercial real estate, and other alternative assets can't be switched up every few microseconds. They need to be nurtured for years. What active means here is an extremely active involvement in selecting alternative investments, which includes a great deal of due diligence in selecting managers. This is only possible for individual investors if they form relationships with expert managers in different alternative asset classes.

Due diligence and risk mitigation are critical to this selection process. Each expert asset-class manager has gone through extensive vetting. This includes visiting home offices and meeting with executives and key management personnel to discover background information and the track records and histories of all current and prior transactions. Legal, accounting, and other compliance officers review these histories and performance metrics, producing in-depth reports. All this due diligence is thoroughly reviewed before offerings are included in any THEM portfolio.

To make alternative private investments, you need hands-on experts on your team who can select and watch these various investments closely, not only because they are extremely knowledgeable about the asset class but because they are involved in these investments through their own money, time, and sweat equity. Their vested interest in these investments is identical to your vested interest. They actively manage investments because they're willing to work to make them successful. They invest their own blood, sweat, and tears, as well as their personal money. One of the key metrics we look for is the sponsors' personal participation in the investments they represent.

Individual investors, however, need more liquidity than institutions like Yale. THEM therefore also finds money managers in public markets who specialize in a single asset class, such as large-cap growth stocks, small-cap value stocks, or certain types of credit—whatever the asset class might be. THEM's underlying philosophy is the same for both private and public investments: a team approach whose members have best-of-class expertise.

## THE VIRTUAL FAMILY OFFICE

Not long ago, this approach was only available outside large institutions to those ultra-wealthy individuals and families able to establish their own "family offices" with full-time financial and legal staff. The members of such families and family offices typically have between $500 million and $10 billion or more in assets they are managing. Their goal is typically one of capital preservation, tax mitigation, estate planning, asset protection, and charitable giving.

Such families could afford to put together family offices encompassing an entire in-house team of investment, legal, accounting, insurance, and other professionals. These investors don't buy into real estate funds. They acquire real estate: buildings that might cost $30 million to $100 million apiece. Their portfolios look like institutional portfolios, even though they are managed "all in the family."

Of course, not all ultra-high-net-worth individuals with family offices inherited their wealth. Some are the "unicorn" entrepreneurs who created the in-demand new products or services that launch and build Fortune 100 businesses, such as Steve Jobs and Mark Zuckerberg—the Rockefellers and Carnegies of our time. They become billionaires when their companies are sold or go public, and they are now able to afford the kind of full-time staff the Rockefellers have had for generations.

However, this family-office approach remains unaffordable for the vast majority of even high-net-worth families. For example, an investor with $5 million in net worth simply doesn't have the resources to hire investment professionals, accountants, and lawyers to work for them full time.

Yet it's now possible for such investors to establish, participate in, and benefit from a "virtual family office." That's what The Household Endowment Model is all about.

## THE WEALTH MANAGER

The COO of The Household Endowment Model's virtual family office is the CEO client's wealth manager. The wealth manager finds the active-investment managers and other professionals a family office would hire full time and delivers their services to the client on a part-time basis. The wealth manager's job is to:

- Assist investor clients in determining what expert services they need in their individual cases.
- Find these experts.
- Manage or quarterback the resulting expert team.

The following diagram illustrates the wealth manager's role in assembling and managing this expert network:

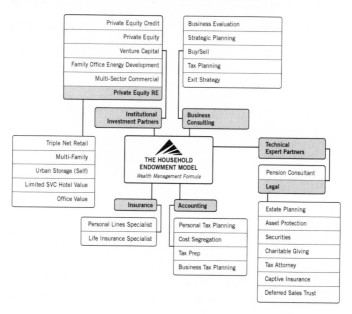

Virtual Family Office Professional Network

The diagram both shows members of the investment-counseling team and anticipates the other legal, accounting, and tax concerns that will be covered in the second part of this book. The underlying principle remains the same. The wealth manager's role in The Household Endowment Model is to create and manage all the different components of the client's virtual family office, including best-of-class investment advisors in a variety of private and public asset classes.

The Household Endowment Model and its virtual family office are late-breaking news. Most investors and investment counselors have no idea this strategy even exists.

Virtual family offices are still a rare and cutting-edge phenomenon. You as an investor, however, now know this new model exists and can be implemented with expert management.

## BEST-OF-CLASS PARTNERSHIPS

The reason that The Household Endowment Model is able to do what it was designed to do—emulate the Yale Endowment investment strategy for individuals and families—is because its investment-management companies have created co-investment programs that high-net-worth families can participate in for tens of thousands rather than millions of dollars. What was required was a way to facilitate such investments outside traditional institutional channels. THEM rises to this challenge by creating co-investments sponsored by best-of-class managers and structured to enable lower buy-in rates.

The wealth manager's quarterbacking job includes finding these managers and developing relationships with them. They are selected on the basis of their extensive, successful track records, and cultivated through professional and personal relationships in which trust develops over the long term.

The wealth manager can trust asset-class managers because they have been selected based on what they do, how they invest, and their philosophies and track records. These private managers, or their companies, typically have anywhere from twenty- to seventy-five-year track records. They've been successfully doing business in their asset classes for a long time.

When a THEM wealth manager is hired to put together a portfolio, the client enters into an established and growing network of such best-of-class managers. Which asset classes the client will invest in is determined first by the general principle of diversification into both private and public assets and then by individual needs determined on a case-by-case basis. THEM has no preset cookie-cutter investment portfolios. Each client's needs are addressed following an extensive discovery process.

These expert managers are given the power to make the investments themselves: to buy, sell, and make other decisions about the assets in their class. THEM, like David Swensen at Yale, believes that expert external managers should be given considerable autonomy to implement strategies as they see fit. They have the in-depth knowledge required, and success depends on their being given the authority to apply it.

### HUB AND SPOKES

The overall point is that The Household Endowment

Model is based upon relationships with experts with a great deal of history and longevity.

It all comes down to a fairly simple question with a simple answer. Do you think you would sleep better at night if you turned your wealth plan over to someone who has access to private money managers who may have been making the same kind of investment for many years and have a stellar long-term track record or to someone who just got started in the last couple of years? The bottom line is that endowment-style investment requires the institutional-style expertise to be found in companies with known, long-term track records, with which the THEM virtual family office has developed long-term relationships.

We just used the sports metaphor of "quarterback" to describe the role of the wealth manager in the virtual-family-office model. Perhaps a better sports metaphor would be not a quarterback or even coach but the general manager who oversees an entire football, baseball, or basketball team. The general manager hires the coaches, who then both recruit and train the team's personnel— including the quarterback. To extend the metaphor, the wealth manager goes out and finds and hires the experts in each asset class, who are in turn authorized and tasked with making the actual investments.

Of course, the term "quarterback" is not entirely inaccurate and probably means more to most people than "general manager." Ultimately, these are just metaphors meant to help convey the role of the wealth manager in a very new and powerful investment strategy, The Household Investment Model.

To get away from sports and into a more concrete image: think of the wealth manager as the hub or center of a wheel and the asset-class and other strategic experts as the spokes radiating out from that hub. Both are necessary if the wheel is to go round. They just have different roles.

Now that all the parts of The Household Endowment Model's alternative investment puzzle have been assembled, it's time to move on to the larger puzzle, of which wealth management and investment counseling are just the first, though very foundational, piece.

Until now, we've focused on investment and, specifically, alternative-investment asset classes. This is linked to the first of the five major concerns of high-net-worth families: wealth preservation. We'll now put this in context and examine the other four primary concerns of affluent families and how THEM addresses each concern.

## PART II

# ADDRESSING YOUR FAMILY'S PRIMARY FINANCIAL CONCERNS

# CHAPTER 6

# THE HOUSEHOLD ENDOWMENT MODEL WEALTH-PLANNING STRATEGY

The way the pieces of an overall wealth strategy fit together won't be a puzzle if the strategy is properly understood and coordinated. Part 1 focused on the cornerstone of this strategy: wealth preservation and investment planning. Part 2 will focus on the other pieces of the wealth-strategy puzzle and how they fit together. Let's take another overview of the entire process before diving more deeply into individual elements.

## INVESTMENT COUNSELING

When you're heading in a new direction, it's always a good idea to pull out your map and reorient yourself. The five major concerns of high-net-worth individuals and families are your wealth-strategy map. You want to maximize the probability that you and your family will achieve your financial goals in five different, now-familiar areas of concern:

**We Understand**

Our Successful Clients'
Most Important
Financial Challenges

1. **Wealth Preservation, Investment Consulting**
   Maximizing the Probability of You Achieving
   All That's Important to You

2. **Wealth Enhancement**
   Mitigating Tax Liability While Helping
   Ensure You Have the Cash Flow You Need

3. **Wealth Transfer**
   The Smoothest, Most Tax-Efficient Way
   to Pass on Your Assets to Your Loved Ones

4. **Wealth Protection**
   Protecting Your Wealth From Creditors, Litigants,
   Potential Lawsuits, and Catastrophic Losses

5. **Charitable Giving**
   Fulfilling Your Charitable Goals in Ways Most
   Beneficial to You and the Causes You Care About

Part 1 focused on wealth preservation and investment counseling, with a stress on the importance of constructing a portfolio diversified beyond the 60/40 model into alternative, non-correlated, private investments. In order to preserve your capital, rather than have the ups and downs of public markets wear it away, your portfolio may need to be stabilized by converting some of your assets from traditional to alternative classes.

Almost all portfolios either follow the straightforward 60/40 model or are variations on the same theme. The big-name, well-established brokerage firms generally allocate most of their clients' assets in publicly traded stocks and bonds. As described below, allocation and reallocation of new THEM clients' assets are made only after extensive consultation and stress-testing of their current portfolios.

What The Household Endowment Model (THEM) then does is convert the typical client portfolio into one that takes advantage of endowment-style investment strategies. The portfolio is designed along the lines of David Swensen's Yale Endowment Model, with the goals of stabilizing assets, mitigating risks, and increasing returns. These alternative investments will not be traded short term but will be given the opportunity to grow, generally over a period of three to seven years.

Since investment counseling does not happen in a vacuum, let's take a step back and look at the process as a whole. To do so, let's return to a graphic first seen a few pages back.

## A COORDINATED TEAM

The Household Endowment Model, like the Yale Endowment, believes in using and giving authority to best-of-class experts in all aspects of wealth management, including and extending beyond investment counseling. The following familiar diagram again illustrates this comprehensive approach:

Virtual Family Office Professional Network

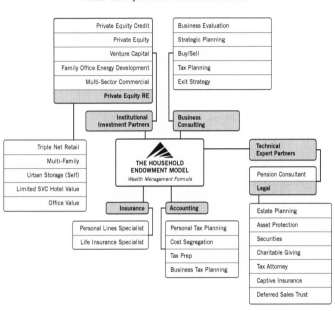

This fully coordinated approach extends the expertise you can draw on beyond specialized investment counselors to the legal, accounting, banking, insurance, and other professionals needed to oversee all aspects of wealth management, including tax planning, estate planning, wealth protection, and charitable giving.

Again, The Household Endowment Model wealth manager is the hub of the wheel, the manager of the entire team of expert specialists working on the client's behalf. The wealth manager is responsible for finding, coordinating, and overseeing the work of all team members, whatever their specialties may be.

## A COMPREHENSIVE FOCUS

THEM has an onboarding process for new clients, using standardized fundamental principles adjusted on a case-by-case basis to individual needs. Transitioning individuals and families to The Household Endowment Model includes planning and execution phases that, while meant to be as efficient as possible, cannot be rushed.

While high-net-worth individuals are almost universally concerned about the five major concerns, each client or prospective client has specific requirements. Everyone is different. Some people want to focus primarily on taking care of their children and grandchildren; others are quite interested in supporting a church or a charitable organization. Conventional wealth managers look primarily, even exclusively, at how to invest clients' money. The Household Endowment Model provides financial solutions to all aspects of the client's lifestyle and family legacy, which are of paramount importance, as well as investment and financial concerns.

Conventional investment advisors aren't concerned with tax or estate planning: ensuring that you save as much of the money you make as possible and that you have the proper wills, trusts, and directives to plan for the future. They don't get involved in protecting your assets or ensuring they won't be taken away from you in an unexpected lawsuit or divorce. Nor do they concern themselves, except at a very high level, with charitable-giving needs. In contrast, THEM covers all these bases.

## PROCESS OVERVIEW

The following chart gives an overview of The Household Endowment Model process:

## The Household Endowment Model
*Wealth Management Formula*

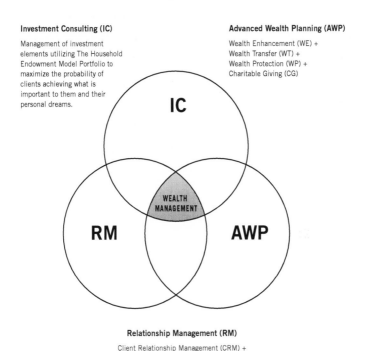

**Investment Consulting (IC)**

Management of investment elements utilizing The Household Endowment Model Portfolio to maximize the probability of clients achieving what is important to them and their personal dreams.

**Advanced Wealth Planning (AWP)**

Wealth Enhancement (WE) +
Wealth Transfer (WT) +
Wealth Protection (WP) +
Charitable Giving (CG)

**Relationship Management (RM)**

Client Relationship Management (CRM) +
Virtual Family Office Relationship Management (VFORM)

This process is fundamentally consultative, of course. It begins with a discovery meeting in which the client's financial and related needs and requirements are discussed and defined. The wealth manager then puts together a proposed investment strategy that is analyzed and modified in an investment-plan meeting that generally takes place about two weeks after the discovery meeting.

At this point, the client and wealth manager confirm

their intention to work together to execute the plan they have devised. That milestone having been reached, the wealth manager begins drawing on THEM's networks of investment, legal, accounting, and other experts in implementing and further refining the agreed-on plan.

Checks, balances, and necessary on-the-ground adjustments are discussed in a series of subsequent conferences. The next major milestone comes about forty-five days after the client and wealth manager have confirmed their intention to work together. This meeting is followed by subsequent regular review meetings at times the client and wealth manager mutually agree upon.

## DISCOVERY AND IMPLEMENTATION

The discovery meeting initiates the entire process. The Household Endowment Model has developed an extensive questionnaire designed to learn as much as possible about prospective clients' requirements and needs: What are the clients' goals? Do they have extensive travel plans and, if so, where, when, and how often? What are their retirement plans? How much debt do they have? What kind of college education are they planning for their children? Will they be taking care of their parents or other relatives? Are they expecting a significant inheritance? And, finally, what's most important to them regarding their money and their legacy?

If the client is a business owner or professional, such as a doctor, in most cases a long-term exit strategy needs to be formulated. Has there been a divorce and second marriage? Are there children from each marriage, how old are they, and what are their current and future needs?

Risk and risk analysis are also taken into account. How much income do clients need now? How much will they need in the future, either for major business projects or retirement? Whether the client has a $500,000, $3 million, or $10 million portfolio, an investment plan is formulated based on liquidity and income needs as well as risk tolerance.

It's critical that clients understand both general principles and their specific application in their own cases. At this point, everyone needs to be given time to pause and consider. Once a proposed investment plan has been presented, clients need time to think about it, sleep on it, and discuss it with family members and other stakeholders. Necessary adjustments are then made, and implementation begins.

Let's now move on to the discussion of the second through fifth of affluent families' five major concerns. We'll go into considerable depth, as we did in covering the first concern, wealth preservation and investment counseling. As you'll see, it's much easier to put the pieces of the puzzle together when you have a better sense of their actual shapes, sizes, and dimensions.

CHAPTER 7

# WEALTH ENHANCEMENT AND TAX MITIGATION

Diversifying your portfolio with alternative investment strategies will potentially both preserve and grow wealth. The second major concern of affluent families is wealth enhancement. An effective approach to enhancing wealth is to mitigate or reduce the amount you pay in taxes, saving as much of your hard-earned cash for yourself as you legally can.

Tax planning is the key to tax mitigation. The problem is that tax and cash-flow planning often take a back seat to or are confused with tax preparation. The two, though related, are very different beasts.

## TAX PLANNING VS. TAX PREPARATION

The Household Endowment Model team includes accountants and CPAs whose focus is wider than you generally encounter. Many CPAs work in areas unconnected to taxes, but probably eight or nine out of ten CPAs who do work in taxes concern themselves almost entirely with tax preparation. While tax preparation is important, tax planning before the final preparation of tax returns is even more so, if you want to enhance your wealth.

The question you should ask yourself is this: Does your current CPA, accountant, or tax preparer only do tax preparation—that is, your tax returns? Or do they also get involved in tax-planning strategies that reduce your taxes? The response is probably "only tax preparation"— and we believe that's the wrong answer. There's much more to tax planning than giving your preparer or accountant your records and receipts in a shoebox and getting back your return to sign and send to the IRS along with a check.

It makes a lot more sense to prepare for tax day by reducing the size of the check you have to write. Most accountants spend most of their time looking in the rearview mirror and almost none looking at how to reduce tax liability, a retrospective rather than prospective process. Tax planning means looking ahead through the windshield as well as the rearview mirror. Tax planning is proactive and tax preparation reactive. Once the end of the year rolls around, it's too late to start planning.

Mesa, Arizona-based Trent Erickson is a highly experienced tax-strategy specialist whose expertise The Household Endowment Model is fortunate to draw upon. His insights and recommendations have greatly contributed to what you are about to learn.

Accountancy and tax law are highly specialized fields that often involve decades of experience. It would be impossible to cover the entire gamut of tax-planning strategies even in several books entirely devoted to the subject. What we'll do here is lay out some general principles illustrated with specific strategies. Think of these as tools in a larger toolbox.

Many high-net-worth individuals are business owners, and certain tax-planning strategies specifically apply to owned-and-operated businesses. While some of those will be touched on here, they'll be covered more fully in the next chapter.

More generally, it's critical to realize that tax planning comes in three varieties: current-year tax planning, next-year tax planning, and long-term tax planning. You'll find an example of long-term planning later in the chapter. Let's focus on the shorter terms first.

## ELIMINATE AND DEFER

Tax planning involves what-if scenarios: What happens if we do such-and-so? What happens to our tax situation if we make this investment? What happens to our tax situation if we make that other investment? Tax planning is all about laying out plausible scenarios and determining in advance what can be done to help you plan for and, wherever legally possible, mitigate your taxes.

These scenarios fall into three categories: eliminating, deferring, and paying your taxes, in that order. The first thing tax planning does is eliminate taxes wherever legally possible. The second is to defer taxes from this to next year or some other future time. Because of the time value of money, it usually makes more sense to pay taxes later rather than sooner whenever possible.

Paying taxes is the last in line. However, the last thing a CPA or other tax planner wants to do is call a client on April 12 and say, "By the way, in three days, you'll owe the IRS $100,000." Those calls are never fun for either party. The third objective of tax planning is to find out, as early as possible, what taxes will be owed and when they will have to be paid to give the client the time to plan.

Tax planners who can tell clients in November and December what they will owe in April are doing their jobs well. Clients may not like what they hear, but at least they have been forewarned and can prepare. In many instances, knowing your "number" or tax liability in October, November, or December gives you the time to explore different tax mitigation strategies to reduce it.

## YOUR NUMBER-ONE EXPENSE

Most people don't really understand that taxes are one the largest expenses they will face in their lifetimes, especially, but not only, if they are business owners. The problem is that most people think about taxes solely in terms of income taxes, which hardly covers the field.

People don't even think about everything their payroll taxes involve. When an employee gets a paycheck with a gross and net amount, they tend to look at what's been taken out as "income tax." Much of the amount, however, is FICA or Social Security and Medicare taxes. Even business owners and employers tend to gloss over the fact that they are also making matching contributions to their employees' FICA and Medicare taxes. Employers also pay unemployment and, in some states, disability taxes. Some states also charge city and municipal taxes.

Sales tax is hardly hidden, but it's not something that people generally think of when calculating the amount of tax they pay during the year. There is now a bit more awareness of this than usual, because online retailers such as Amazon are gradually being required to pay sales tax in more states. Still, few people calculate or even think about how much sales tax they actually pay in the course of a year.

Then there are personal property taxes, which homeowners are certainly aware of but tend to get shunted to a different category from income-tax liability. Most people also pay a tax on their automobiles when it comes time to register them every year. Businesses pay additional annual property taxes on any buildings they own, as well as annual property taxes on their furniture, fixtures, and equipment.

The point is that when you start adding all these taxes up—income tax, payroll tax, sales tax, real property tax, personal property tax—you quickly come to realize how large a percentage of your income is going to taxes. The importance of tax planning now starts to come into focus.

Having drawn your attention to this unpleasant news, it's time to delve into some of the strategies that exist for legally eliminating or deferring taxes: the tricks of the trade that genuine tax planners carry around in their briefcases.

## COST SEGREGATION

Cost segregation is a tool people who own commercial real estate, one of the principal alternative asset classes, can use to defer taxes. If you own a commercial office building and lease it out to someone else's company, or even your own, the building is depreciated over thirty-nine and a half years. However, you can accelerate depreciation on some parts of the building if they are properly identified and segregated.

For instance, the carpeting and window coverings in an office building might have a five-year rather than an almost forty-year depreciation life span. The IRS also considers what cost-segregation experts call "qualified" electrical and plumbing to have a five- or seven-year life span. A cost-segregation study may also determine that the building's exterior assets, such as a parking lot, have a fifteen-year life span. A cost-segregation study that breaks a property down into these different parts can dramatically defer taxes by identifying more depreciation up front and less down the road.

## DEFERRED SALES TRUST

A Deferred Sales Trust (DST) is a tool that can be used by any taxpayer facing a large capital gain. It doesn't matter where that capital gain occurs. It could be from the sale of a business, real estate, highly appreciated stock, or an artwork.

A Deferred Sales Trust is just that: you establish a trust, managed by a trustee, and sell the assets that have appreciated, or will appreciate, to that trust prior to the assets' being sold to a third party. When you sell the assets to the trustee, the trustee gives you a note receivable. What you now own is the note receivable rather than the assets themselves.

The note is similar to a mortgage. How many times do you think to yourself that you own your house? If, as is usually the case, you have a mortgage on the house, the bank or mortgage-holder actually owns it.

A DST works similarly. You sell your assets into the trust and, rather than directly owning the assets in the trust, you own a note against those assets.

This permits you to defer paying taxes on the sale of the assets, since the IRS distinguishes between an outright and an installment sale. Internal Revenue Code 453 allows you to pay taxes on a capital gain only at the time you take money out of the trust, which you can do incrementally.

Any highly appreciated asset is eligible to be bought and sold through a Deferred Sales Trust. We'll look at what this specifically means for selling a business in the next chapter.

What's called a 1031 Exchange, from IRS code section 1031, is a tax-deferral tool similar to a Deferred Sales Trust. It's also known as a Delaware Statutory Trust, although 1031 Exchange is easier to say. This is a deferral tool that can be used if you own commercial or residential rental property.

Rather than taking the capital gains from the sale of the rental property, you can reinvest them into a 1031 Exchange, which basically enables you to purchase another rental property while deferring capital gains taxes on the last one. This process, which allows you to defer capital gains taxes while building your portfolio, can continue indefinitely. Of course, as with all tax planning, before acting, you should check with your tax professional to understand all the facets of this strategy.

## OPPORTUNITY ZONE INVESTMENTS

The Tax Cuts and Jobs Act signed into law in 2017 establishes another means of deferring capital gains taxes by investing in "Opportunity Zones." Opportunity Zones are specially designated, economically distressed areas in need of investment and rehabilitation. There are several tax advantages to investing capital gains in an Opportunity Zone.

Many run-down commercial and residential areas

throughout the country desperately need reinvestment dollars. The US Treasury Department went to the governors of each state and asked them to identify the areas in their states in need of redevelopment. The governors submitted lists of such areas, and the Treasury Department certified those that qualified as Opportunity Zones.

It should also be noted that not all properties in Opportunity Zones are necessarily what are thought of as "run-down areas." Some properties just happen to fall within zip codes the state governor has identified in this manner.

The upshot is that if you realize a capital gain, you have six months to invest that money in an Opportunity Zone in order to reap the investment's tax advantages. The first inducement is that an Opportunity Zone investment defers your capital-gain taxes until 2026.

Let's take a concrete example. Say you buy a rental house in an Opportunity Zone for $150,000. To qualify for a capital gains deferral, you need to spend another $150,000 renovating that house. With this investment, you've now deferred taxes on a $300,000 capital gain until 2026.

Capital gains tax deferral is the first of three benefits of getting into an Opportunity Zone investment. As long as you hold that investment, you don't have to pay capital gains tax until 2026. If you sell that investment before 2026, you'll need to pay capital gains tax when you do.

The second benefit of an Opportunity Zone investment is a reduction in the amount of the tax you pay. If you hold the new investment for five years, you get a step-up in basis on the original asset, thereby reducing your capital gains tax by as much as 10 percent. If you hold the investment an additional two years, for a total of seven years, you get an additional 5 percent step-up in basis, reducing your tax even further.

The third, final, and probably greatest benefit of an Opportunity Zone investment is that if you hold it for a minimum of ten years, you pay no capital gains tax at all on the money you make when you sell the investment. Again: you've invested $300,000 in the rental property and have held it for ten years. Let's say you sell it in year eleven for $400,000. You will then pay no capital gains tax at all on the $100,000 profit you've made on the sale. However, again, as with all tax planning, you should check with your tax professional to understand all this strategy's facets.

## ROTH CONVERSION: LONG-TERM TAX PLANNING

Earlier on, we mentioned that there is this-year tax planning, next-year tax planning, and long-term tax planning. Let's look at an example of long-term planning.

First, you should realize that long-term tax planning may increase your short-term tax liability. While this may seem crazy at first, it actually makes good sense to give up a little today to get a lot back tomorrow. This is what happens with a Roth Conversion.

If you have money in a regular IRA or 401(k) account transferred to an IRA, you'll pay income tax when you take money out of the account after you retire. You don't pay taxes if you take money out of a Roth IRA account because the money in a Roth IRA consists of after-tax dollars. With a regular IRA, you get tax deductions for the years you put money in.

There are a number of private investments, particularly in commercial and multifamily residential real estate, that offer an IRS-approved discounted value when converting from a regular into a Roth IRA. Say toward the end of one year you invest $100,000 from a regular IRA in an investment property in the developmental stage. At the end of the year, the developer is required to have a third-party, independent appraisal done on the current value of the investment.

Then, early the following year, the custodian of your regular IRA is required to tell you the fair market value of your IRA on the last day of the previous year. The development you've invested in, however, is now just raw land, sticks, and bricks. The building or buildings haven't been built, and there are no tenants. As a result, the current fair market value of your investment may be as low as 50 percent of the original investment. In plain English: your $100,000 investment is now worth $50,000.

After you've been talked down from your panic, thinking you've lost half your money, you will realize that you've got an opportunity here. You can convert the investment from a regular IRA to a Roth IRA and now pay taxes on a valuation of $50,000 rather than $100,000.

Fast forward four or five years. The property has now been developed, and the buildings sold off. Your original $100,000 investment could now potentially be worth $150,000—all of which, being in a Roth IRA, is now tax-free. With a Roth Conversion, you're actually paying some tax dollars now because you want to save a lot of tax dollars in the future. Like "insider trading" on private investments, this isn't illegal. It's perfectly legal and very smart.

Also, now that you have converted this asset to a Roth IRA, all future investments made after this asset's sale will grow tax-free. This conversion, it's important to note, is available to all IRA owners and is not subject to any income or other restrictions.

The most important lesson here is that tax mitigation depends on this-year, next-year, and long-term tax planning. Plan ahead!

And planning ahead is even more important when you're building a business you intend to sell.

# CHAPTER 8

# BUSINESS OWNERSHIP AND EXIT STRATEGY

We interrupt this program...

Actually, we're not really interrupting our program of going through wealthy families' major concerns. We're just pausing to deal specifically with the concerns of an important category of high-net-worth individuals: successful business owners. If you have founded, are building, and intend to sell your business, you're about to find out how The Household Endowment Model has you covered.

## THE BUSINESS OWNER'S DILEMMA

If you're a business owner, your attention is sharply focused on running and growing your enterprise. Most of your assets are probably tied up in your business. The problem is that you may not have the bandwidth or expertise to manage your net worth so as to protect and maximize it for you and your family.

You are probably building your business with the intention of selling it at a handsome profit someday. That's your retirement plan. However, you can't wait until the day before you decide to sell to say, "Okay, I'm going to sell my business tomorrow." If you don't want to give up a large percentage of your profit to taxes, you have to plan for the sale years in advance. Selling your business requires preparing and executing an intricate transition process.

People generally build businesses for three reasons. The first two are that they 1) want to provide a good lifestyle for themselves and their families and 2) don't want to work for someone else. The best way to attain both goals is to build and grow a business of your own.

The third goal is to build your business for eventual sale at considerable profit. As your business becomes more successful, you need to pay attention to the details of both your personal net worth and the business's value. You'll also want to be prepared for any unanticipated occurrences, including lawsuits or similar catastrophes that could threaten the security of your enterprise.

Welcome to the world of multitasking. Fortunately, you can now outsource this to The Household Endowment Model and its team of experts. Of course, you'll remain involved in planning, but you can now delegate important details and decisions with confidence. Your main focus will remain your business, as it should, but you'll have the other critical bases covered.

We're not talking only about business owners in the traditional sense here. Many if not most of the physicians, dentists, and similar professionals who build their own practices are also building businesses and need to plan their exit strategies.

## BUSINESS AND PERSONAL ASSETS

Perhaps the key to planning an exit strategy is separating your business and personal assets while gradually transferring as many assets as possible from the business to the personal column. To repeat, business owners usually hold most of their assets in their enterprises. That may be necessary when first starting a business, but this approach becomes increasingly self-defeating as the business grows.

Let's use a simple analogy. If you're a business owner, think of your financial life as being like a pair of pants. Say your business assets are in the front left pocket and your personal or individual assets in the front right pocket. There are two pockets but one pair of pants: all your assets are in one pocket or the other.

The basic principle is, whenever possible, to move assets from the front left to the front right pocket—from the business to the personal side. Of course, it's a bit more complicated than that. You may need to move some assets to a side or back pocket, depending on which strategies, such as tax mitigation, are used to protect your personal wealth.

These are all different pockets in the same pair of pants. The money isn't being taken away but getting moved around so that you can keep as much of the profits you make as possible when selling your business. If you keep all your assets in your front left pocket, you may have to pay up to half your profits in tax when selling your business, and that's obviously what you want to avoid.

## START EARLY

It's worth noting that moving assets from the operating business "pocket," where they are liabilities, to the personal "pocket," where they are protected, will also help preserve your assets in the shorter term. This also means that, while it's never too late to start exit planning, it's always better to start early.

Many Household Endowment Model clients are business owners or independent professionals in their forties or fifties. They're relatively young and not thinking about how they're going to sell and get out of their businesses. An exit strategy may never cross their minds, but it should.

Actually, they should be thinking about an exit from day one. When you start a business, you should immediately start considering how and when you will leave. Do you want to sell your business, making it your retirement plan? Do you want to turn it over to the next generation? If so, are there members of the next generation with both the desire and ability to take it over?

The simple rule is not to put all your eggs in one basket. If all your wealth is tied up in your business, and something happens to it, there goes all your wealth. The underlying Household Endowment Model principle, here as else-where, is diversification. As a business owner, you need to begin taking some of the wealth and assets invested in the business and put it into other investments as soon as possible. Doing so will give you greater long-term security.

To use a now-familiar term, these assets should be non-correlated to the business, just as your portfolio should include private investments non-correlated to public markets. Indeed, one of the best places to invest these assets is possibly in a personalized THEM portfolio.

## DON'T LET THIS HAPPEN TO YOU

Having an exit strategy in place and diversifying your assets through the years will protect you as a business owner. To drive the point home, let's take the example of a medical professional who has done very well financially, making between $500,000 and $1 million a year, year in and year out, for many years. A low year for him would probably be $600,000 in net income, and a really good year would be $1 million.

He's now in his early sixties and has no money set aside for retirement. Every penny he's earned throughout his career has been used to build and support a high-end lifestyle. He lives in a $2.5-million-to-$3-million home, on which he still has a $1-million mortgage. He has a nice second home, an upscale cabin in the country, with an equally healthy mortgage. He and his family are always going on wonderful vacations. All his earnings have gone to support this lifestyle.

This is an intelligent man who hasn't applied his smarts to thinking about retirement. He figures that he has a business he will be able to sell for $3 million to $4 million, so everything will be all right. Going through the numbers, however, brings home the fact that even if he sells the business for $4 million, that capital is not going to generate the $600,000 to $1 million in yearly income to which he's become accustomed.

This is a big wake-up call, and what he needs to wake up to is an even bigger nightmare. He realizes it's possible that, given market conditions, he may not be able to sell his practice for as much as he'd like. Since his sole asset is his business, he's going to be in a lot of trouble if he retires, as originally planned, in three years.

It's never too late to start doing things differently, but timing is not in his favor. If he had begun participating in The Household Endowment Model Wealth Planning Strategies five or ten years earlier, he may have been much better prepared for retirement without a dramatic reduction in lifestyle. For instance, he's been paying between $200,000 to $400,000 a year in income tax, which could have been cut in half with the right investment strategy.

## CAPTIVE INSURANCE

Another tool business owners can use to eliminate or defer income tax prior to exit is what's called captive insurance. This is a complex subject, but we can hit some highlights and basic principles here.

For some time, large businesses have been taking advantage of captive insurance companies—insurance companies the businesses themselves establish to cover or self-insure selected risks. These "captives" enable large businesses to customize coverage to their individual needs and get greater control over insurance costs and claims-handling. This customized insurance coverage allows a business to insure risks for which commercial insurance coverage is either unavailable or impractical.

In the past, establishing and maintaining captive insurance was cost-prohibitive for any but the very largest companies. The good news is this has changed. In 2008, the IRS issued a ruling that allows a core captive insurance company to be set up and then divided into semi-autonomous "cells," each of which is owned by different companies. Think of "captive cells" as a way for small and medium-sized businesses to work together to participate in the benefits of captive insurance at a fraction of the cost. For our purposes, we will refer to these captive cells as a captive insurance company or simply a captive.

Let's look at three of captives' numerous benefits. First, they can save a business money on insurance premiums.

Second, they allow smaller businesses to insure against risks their other policies do not, and cannot, cover. Third, a business owner pays tax-deductible premiums from their regular operating company to the captive insurance company they also own.

Those premiums are used to pay claims. However, premiums used to pay claims can also become the captive's profit. Best of all, this profit typically has a tax rate of zero percent (0 percent). That was not a typo, nor is it a tax loophole. Congress specifically set forth tax benefits that are typical of all insurance companies for captives, allowing them to accumulate premiums and reserves to pay claims. These benefits allow insurance companies, including captives, to build insurance reserves. At the same time, business owners can build real assets in the captive insurance companies they also own.

A captive is sometimes compared to a type of retirement plan without all the rules and restrictions, but this appealing comparison is also simplistic. Business owners do get a tax deduction while building the asset, just as they do when building a retirement plan. The key difference is that the asset is in the form of a captive insurance company that covers real business risks, which a retirement plan does not.

There are several reasons this asset can be a key component of a business owner's long-term financial well-being. First, the tax deductions for the operating company and the tax-free treatment of the captive's profits are an efficient way of building insurance reserves. Second, when the insured operating company has a loss covered by the captive, these insurance reserves will be available to pay the claim, which is very helpful when needed. In the case of a large or catastrophic business-casualty loss, these insurance reserves can save the enterprise. Third, as previously mentioned, a captive can build value over time, which will be available to the business owner upon eventual exit from the business.

You were warned that this is a complicated subject. Fortunately, we don't need to go into more detail here, since best-of-breed insurance advice is available through The Household Endowment Model expert team.

## THE DOMESTIC INTERNATIONAL SALES CORPORATION

A Domestic International Sales Corporation or DISC, which is sometimes referred to as a Foreign Sales Corporation, is another tool that can eliminate business taxes. A DISC allows businesses with international sales to eliminate certain taxes on export income. If your business exports products or services internationally, a DISC can help eliminate a large portion of US tax on this income.

The Internal Revenue Code gives significant tax incentives for export activities to domestic corporations, that is, business enterprises incorporated in the United States. DISC shareholders, such as business owners, benefit from greatly reduced income tax rates on the income earned from certain exports of US-produced goods. If your business exports goods internationally, you would benefit from the advice on creating a DISC available through The Household Endowment Model expert team.

## RETURN OF THE DST

A Deferred Sales Trust (DST) is an important tax-deferment tool discussed in the previous tax-strategy chapter. It's also a good tool to use when planning and executing a business exit. The proceeds from a sale can be put in a DST, which has several advantages, beginning with tax deferment. In a recent case, a business owner who had just sold his business would have had to pay $600,000 in income tax if the profits from the sale had not been put in a DST.

A DST doesn't eliminate this tax, but, because it defers it, that $600,000 can now be invested, along with the former business owner's other assets. Taxes can be deferred, and return from the investment realized, for any number of years. In some cases, tax can even be eliminated if the trust remains in place after the owner's death, since the assets in the trust will then pass on to the business owner's beneficiaries.

More on this in the next chapter on wealth transfer and estate planning. For now, let's just say that a DST's main purpose in an exit strategy is as a tax-deferral tool.

## EXIT STRATEGIES

The business-exit strategies you've just learned about are illustrative rather than exhaustive. The Household Endowment Model provides access to tax, insurance, and pension experts who have devoted their entire careers to utilizing established and innovating new business-owner wealth-preservation strategies.

Another tool is utilizing the tax advantages of hiring your own children. You can pay them through your company payroll, and they can then invest that money in an IRA. That means you can write off what you paid them, and they can write off what they put into their IRAs. Taxes are significantly deferred or eliminated, creating another way for you to pass money from your business to your children.

The takeaway here is that if you are a business owner, you should always plan for and keep your exit strategy in mind. It may never be too late to plan, but earlier is always better.

Also bear in mind that your exit strategy will keep changing and evolving. Times change, tax laws change, and the economic environment changes. The earlier you begin planning your exit strategy, the more it may change over time, and this should be seen as a net positive, since it increases your level of control.

It's now time to resume our regular programming, beginning with the third of the five major concerns of affluent families, which we've briefly touched on in this chapter: wealth transfer and estate planning.

# CHAPTER 9

# WEALTH TRANSFER AND ESTATE PLANNING

What is going to happen to the wealth you have accumulated should you have the bad judgment to pass away?

High-net-worth individuals and families, who may be very sophisticated at business, are often surprisingly unsophisticated about even the basics of estate planning. An even larger number continually put off making plans for their estate, sometimes until it is too late. Making and executing a plan take time and effort, but it's time and effort well spent.

Let's not fool ourselves by pretending that it is easy or pleasant to think about, much less plan for, your inevitable demise. However, as with the sale of a business, it's always better to start planning earlier than later. Remember the old saying that Benjamin Franklin—who else?—is believed to have first come up with in 1789: "In this world, nothing can be said to be certain, except death and taxes."

## DRAWING UP YOUR WILL

The laws that govern how your assets will be disposed of after your death vary from state to state and change over time. The greater your accumulated assets, the greater the effect these laws will have. That's why it's important to have access to the legal advice of the experts on your THEM team.

The underlying principle is that you want to determine what will happen to your assets after your death. If you don't take steps to do this, not you, but the laws of your state will make those determinations. That is what you want to avoid by planning ahead.

It's likely that you want your assets to go to your spouse after you die. That provision is generally written into state law. However, what if you and your spouse die at the same time in an accident of some kind? Your assets will probably pass to your children, if you have children, but what if you don't? Or what if you want certain assets to go to certain children and other assets to go to other people or institutions? If that isn't written down in black and white in a will, your wishes will not have the weight of law behind them.

The first step in estate planning is drawing up a will. If you die intestate—that is, without having formulated a will—a court will determine who is entitled to inherit your assets and how. This is what you want, above all, to avoid.

Let's take a trivial example. Say you own a Rolex watch and a Timex. Who gets the Rolex? Who gets the Timex? Who gets neither? More generally, who is entitled to what part of your assets, and who is not entitled to anything?

Also, it's critical to be aware of and account for the fact that a will only applies to assets in your own name. If you and a business partner have a joint checking account, on your death the assets in the account will revert to your surviving business partner, not to your own estate.

## ESTABLISHING A TRUST

Your will, if you have one, will be probated once you have the bad judgment to die. The Dictionary.com definition of probate is "the official proving of a will." In other words, even if you've written a will, it needs to be legally validated, and this is generally done in a probate court. In this case, the court decides not how your assets should be distributed according to the laws of your state but whether the instructions you have set forth in your will are legally valid. This is generally the case, but it is also possible for the heir who got the Timex watch rather than the Rolex to contest the terms of your will.

A book titled *How to Avoid Probate* was published and became a best seller many years ago. Since then, the probate process has been simplified and made less onerous. However, the underlying principle remains valid: not only do you not want to die intestate, but you want to avoid probate as much as you can. The best way to do this is to establish a trust.

Trusts come in many different varieties; we've already looked at real estate investment trusts and DSTs or Deferred Sales Trusts. Trusts are basically legal entities to which you can transfer your assets. Once this is done, the trust, rather than you as an individual, now own and control these assets. This transfer of ownership can have many legal, tax, and other benefits.

In the case of wealth transfer, you want to establish a living trust, which means a trust that continues to "live" after you die. If this trust owns your business, house, or other real estate and investment assets, it retains ownership of those assets even after you die.

In establishing the trust, you have the authority to incorporate directives as to how the trust should deal with those assets. To avoid confusion, understand that a will cannot own anything and controls only assets held in an individual's name at death. A trust is a legal entity capable of owning assets. Essentially, your directives incorporate the instructions in your will into the trust. They turn your will into an integral part of the living trust.

These directives specify how you want your assets to be handled. Say the trust is drawn up while you still own your business. Should you die before the business is sold or otherwise transferred, your directives can state exactly what you want done with the business. Who should take it over and run it? How much ownership should so-and-so have? Should someone who might have inherited the business if you had died intestate receive no ownership position at all?

The same is true of your real estate, investments, and other assets—not only who gets the Rolex and who gets the Timex but who gets the house. If you have several children, should one of them inherit your primary residence? Or should it be sold, and all your children receive an equal share of the profits?

Many directives in a trust are standard legal "boilerplate," meaning they are the same in most or almost all such trusts. However, there are always specific, individual circumstances. Say that you have children who are still minors. Should they be entitled to an inheritance immediately after your death or only after turning twenty-one? Do you feel, for whatever reason, that they would be better served if they waited until a while longer, say until age thirty, to come into their inheritance?

In the final analysis, a trust is a particularly effective tool for protecting your assets for your beneficiaries, such as your children. It is they, as your beneficiaries, who will benefit the most from the trust.

## DESIGNATING A TRUSTEE

A trust essentially allows you to retain control of your assets from beyond the grave. You and your spouse will generally be the executors of a living trust while you are still alive. You should also designate a successor trustee to take over administration of the trust upon your death.

Whoever you appoint as trustee should, quite literally, be someone you know you can trust. The trustee should be someone whose judgment and honesty you rely on, and who is willing to follow the directives you have set out in the trust. A trustee does not have to be a financial or legal expert, because they can hire lawyers, accountants, and investment advisors to give them expert assistance when necessary. All this is built into The Household Endowment Model's best-of-class team structure.

The trustee does need to know the trust's beneficiaries fairly well in order, for example, to determine if a distribution not specifically required in the trust should be made. They should communicate frequently with the beneficiaries, provide timely and necessary information, and answer questions.

## MEDICAL DIRECTIVES

Before we get into ways of using trusts to legally protect your assets from taxes and other liabilities, let's return to you personally. Since it's likely that you will become ill before you pass away, it's critical that your trust contain a medical directive as well as financial ones.

The cornerstone of a healthcare directive is conferring medical power of attorney on someone you trust to make medical decisions for you. To clarify, power of attorney permits someone else to act on your behalf and in your interests while you are still alive. The individual given your medical power of attorney may or may not be the person you have designated as trustee of your living trust.

Your health may be such that, while you are still alive, you become incapacitated and therefore unable to make decisions about medical care for yourself. Granting medical power of attorney to, for example, one of your children gives them the authority to make these decisions for you.

Your medical directive can place restrictions on these decisions, of course. You can specify how long you want to be on a life support system, such as a ventilator, if you are in a terminal condition or persistent vegetative state. For as long as possible or only for so long and no longer? You can also specify whether or not you want to be resuscitated if you go into a coma. You may wish to specify whether you want to become an organ donor on your demise. On the other hand, you might prefer to leave one or more of these decisions entirely up to the person with your medical power of attorney, trusting them to act in your best interests when you're no longer capable of making decisions for yourself.

## IRREVOCABLE TRUSTS AND TAX MITIGATION

The terms of a living trust can be changed, amended, or revoked up to the time of your death. An irrevocable trust, on the other hand, is a trust where assets you have deposited cannot be retrieved during your lifetime, nor its terms changed, at least not easily. To simplify a complex legal matter: one reason to establish an irrevocable trust is to mitigate the taxes your heirs might otherwise be required to pay on your assets after you pass away.

Let's take one tax-mitigation strategy as an example. Say your estate is worth $10 million. The concern is that your heirs will have to pay several million of those dollars in taxes when you die.

One solution to this problem is to create an irrevocable trust into which you place, say, $100,000 or more. The trust, not you as an individual, can then buy a life insurance policy naming you as the insured. Premiums on the policy will be paid as necessary from the funds in the trust. While you are the insured, the irrevocable life-insurance trust is the policy owner, since you no longer have any control over the assets in the trust. Then, when you have the bad judgment to die, the life-insurance benefits are paid into the trust.

Your heirs will then become the beneficiaries of the life-insurance policy the trust owns. Since not you but the trust owns the policy, these life-insurance benefits are not included as part of your estate. The end result is that your heirs are now entitled to receive those benefits tax-free.

To put the matter in round figures, say your estate is $10 million and the benefits from your life-insurance policy are another $10 million. When you die, your estate will be worth $10 million, rather than $20 million, since the $10 million in benefits is controlled by an irrevocable trust, which paid the premiums on the policy while you were still alive. The benefits of the policy then go directly to its beneficiaries, who will also most probably be the heirs of your estate.

This is one example of many different types of trusts and trust strategies that exist and have specific tax and other advantages. Again, lawyers who specialize in trusts and estate law spend their entire careers focusing on this complex subject, so it's impossible to cover it in depth here.

The key message is to make sure that you've put your financial house in order by establishing a living trust and, if appropriate, an irrevocable trust. In doing so, it's wise to work with the legal and financial professionals THEM provides access to, such as estate-planning attorneys who have the expertise to explore all the options for legally protecting your wealth from taxes and other liabilities.

## LAST WORDS

A living trust is just that: a living document. It can't just be drawn up and set aside. It needs to be reviewed and updated from time to time. Say you draw up the trust, as you should, while you still own a business. The trust will need to be revised when and if the business is sold. Say your oldest child is still in elementary school when the trust is first drawn. Once your youngest child turns twenty-one, the directives in the trust will undoubtedly need to be revised.

The truth, however unfortunate, is that Benjamin Franklin, as usual, was right about death and taxes. At some point, you and your spouse will have the bad judgment to pass away. What then happens can remain largely in your control, but only if you take concerted and realistic action.

Such action can also be taken to protect your assets from lawsuits and other potential liabilities. Not everyone you come into contact with is going to be scrupulous. Let's have a look at the measures The Household Endowment Model can take to help shield you and your wealth from these pitfalls.

# CHAPTER 10

# WEALTH AND ASSET PROTECTION

We live in a litigious society, and wealthy individuals and families are primary targets for lawsuits. It really can be a jungle out there, so affluent families' fourth major concern is protecting their wealth from potential lawsuits, litigants, creditors, and catastrophic loss.

Of course, anyone can be sued, and the legal fees and other expenses needed to defend against even unfounded or nuisance lawsuits often involve financial loss. Given their "deep pockets," high-net-worth individuals are more likely than others to be targeted.

## THE ASSET-PROTECTION STRESS TEST

Asset protection is a critical component of any wealth-planning strategy. You need to create barriers that will protect your wealth. The Household Endowment Model therefore incorporates asset protection as part of its overall wealth-management strategy.

There are universal general principles behind any good asset-protection plan, but these need to be adapted to individual needs. One way to get moving in the right direction is to take a four-step stress test of your current asset-protection plan, or lack thereof. This test will help you determine how well your wealth is now shielded from frivolous or unfounded lawsuits and similar attacks.

The four steps in the asset-protection stress test are these:

1. Determine high-probability, significant risks: What is likely to happen, and, if it does happen, how detrimental will it be? This can be a rough estimate based on your experience or involve more sophisticated analysis and calculation.
2. Determine your level of concern: What are your needs, wants, and issues? For instance, if you are involved in a business whose products and services are cutting-edge and experimental, your level of concern might be higher than if you own a more conventional business.
3. Evaluate your current asset-protection plan: Do you have a plan at all and, if you do, is it adequate to your needs?

4. Take appropriate action: This may involve taking dramatic next steps or, if all is well, no steps at all. Integrating The Household Endowment Model into your overall wealth-management strategy may be one such appropriate strategy.

## PROTECT YOUR WEALTH BY AVOIDING MISTAKES

Asset-protection planning uses legally accepted strategies to ensure your wealth is not taken from you unjustly. These strategies can help avoid litigation entirely or can help motivate an amicable settlement should litigation take place.

Legitimate asset protection has nothing to do with hiding assets or any other illegal or unethical practice. However, asset protection can be a somewhat tricky business, so the best way to protect yourself is by avoiding pitfalls and mistakes.

There are five major mistakes affluent individuals and families often make that expose their assets to litigants, creditors, and other potentially devastating consequences:

1. Starting to protect your assets when it's already too late
2. Not having liability insurance

3. Not integrating asset protection with your other wealth-management strategies
4. Being unsure of why you have made or are making important decisions
5. Not seeking professional guidance

To help you protect your wealth as much as you can, let's look at how to avoid each of these mistakes in turn.

## FIRST MISTAKE: STARTING TOO LATE

If you haven't done so already, the time to start asset-protection planning is *now*. The time *not* to start is once you are aware that a claim is or may be made against you.

The legal term for moving assets into a trust or other vehicle to protect them after you know or suspect a claim may be made against you is "fraudulent conveyance." In court, any attempt at fraudulent conveyance will be reversed and probably make a bad situation even worse.

Fraudulent conveyance comes in two varieties:

- Actual fraud: This involves actual intent. It occurs when someone transfers assets to a third party who is under their control or influence. This strategy is to make it seem that you no longer have the assets necessary to pay creditors or litigants, although those assets are actually still under your control.

- Constructive fraud: This involves the economics of a transfer of assets rather than the intent behind the transfer. If someone in financial difficulty transfers assets rapidly or precipitously, there may be a presumption of constructive fraud.

Determining intent is tricky, since it is often impossible to know exactly what someone was thinking or intending. As a way of getting around this difficulty, courts look at circumstantial evidence or what are called "badges of fraud," which include the following:

- Current or likely litigation
- Transfer of assets to family members
- Transfers conducted secretly

The solution to this problem is to do asset-protection planning before you need the protection. Don't delay. If you haven't acted yet, act now.

## SECOND MISTAKE: NO LIABILITY INSURANCE

This mistake comes in a number of variations: no liability insurance, not enough liability insurance, or the wrong kind of liability insurance.

This is a simple problem with a simple solution. Many individuals—even highly competent, successful business owners—have no or substandard liability insurance. They could benefit from larger umbrella liability policies, but neither they nor their insurance brokers have taken this into consideration. Certain insurance companies also limit the amount of liability coverage that can be provided.

Effective asset-protection planning requires ensuring that you have the right kinds and amounts of liability insurance. Most people could, for instance, benefit from larger umbrella liability policies, but neither they nor their brokers think of or consider this. A further complication is that many, although not all, insurance companies limit the amount of liability insurance their brokers can provide.

The good news is that liability insurance is relatively inexpensive. You and your wealth manager simply need to seek out the right insurer and the right policy. Business owners in particular might benefit from a higher-quality or more customized "D&O" ("directors and officers") liability plan.

The first line of defense in an asset-protection plan is to avoid lawsuits, although this is often out of your control. The second line of defense is adequate liability insurance. To determine if your liability insurance meets your needs, take or retake the stress test set forth earlier in this chapter. This should be done and redone at regular intervals to uncover and correct any gaps in coverage, since circumstances are bound to change.

## THIRD MISTAKE: NOT INTEGRATING ASSET PROTECTION WITH OTHER WEALTH-MANAGEMENT STRATEGIES

As we've said many times, comprehensive wealth management and planning encompass all five major concerns, including estate planning and tax mitigation. Unfortunately, the various components of an overall strategy are often approached separately and independently, which is exactly the wrong way around.

The Household Endowment Model was specifically created to take a holistic approach to all aspects of wealth management, ensuring that all components of your financial life work together seamlessly. Such an approach leads to and includes an understanding of trade-offs that are being made and risks that might otherwise have been overlooked.

A good example is gifting heirs: This might be good estate planning but could be considered a fraudulent conveyance when it comes to asset protection. Preventing such problems requires the care and coordination that can only come with a wider perspective.

For example, placing inherited assets in a properly structured trust can protect them from creditors, such as divorcing spouses. Here, two of the five major concerns, estate planning and asset protection, have been made to work hand-in-hand. In almost every case, comprehensive wealth-management solutions are both more effective and cost-effective than piecemeal ones.

## FOURTH MISTAKE: BEING UNSURE OF WHY YOU HAVE MADE OR ARE MAKING IMPORTANT DECISIONS

Why have you made certain asset-protection-planning decisions? What was your rationale, and what was the intended result? If you can't answer these questions, there is a good chance that your asset-protection planning will not deliver the actual protection you need. In a legal deposition, for instance, there is a strong possibility a court will be suspicious if you can't give good answers to these questions.

There's an important proviso here, which is that you need to be able to answer such questions on a general, rather than specific, level. Asset-protection planning can become quite complex if your financial and personal circumstances are complicated, as they often are with high-net-worth individuals.

You should be able to explain the reasoning behind the

actions you have taken in broad terms, but you don't need to be an expert in the strategies and financial products that have been employed. That's up to the skilled professionals whose advice you have solicited and followed, which leads to the fifth asset-protection mistake you should avoid.

## FIFTH MISTAKE: NOT SEEKING PROFESSIONAL GUIDANCE

To protect your assets, as is the case in meeting all your wealth-management needs, you need to work with skilled professionals. The problem is that many who say they are asset-protection-planning professionals don't really have the expertise they claim.

Some of these so-called experts are pretenders who know just enough about asset-protection strategies to get themselves and you into trouble. Others could be called predators, because they prey on fear of litigation but deliver ineffectual solutions. There is a third category, exploiters, who overcharge egregiously for asset-protection solutions that may well be inappropriate. All these categories of so-called experts will end up doing you far more harm than good.

You need to work with a true authority in the field of asset-protection planning, someone other financial professionals recognize as an expert. This goes hand-in-hand with integrating asset protection into a holistic wealth-management strategy. Again, The Household Endowment Model has been created precisely to give you access to an interconnected network of such genuine professionals.

It's possible to escape the jungle out there by taking appropriate action. There's another point to be made here. The world we live in is much more than a jungle, which is why the fifth major concern of many affluent families is charitable giving.

# CHAPTER 11

# CHARITABLE GIVING

Steve Jobs once said, "We're here to put a dent in the universe. Otherwise, why else even be here?" Everyone who wants to put a dent in the universe does so in his or her own way. Charitable giving is one of the most effective and beneficial ways of widening your influence. It also enables you to do well by doing good.

## PURPOSE AND PLANNING

An overwhelming majority of affluent individuals make charitable donations as a way of giving back. A BSW (Becoming Seriously Wealthy) Inner Circle poll asked 247 highly successful business owners why they wanted to be wealthier. Nearly three-quarters—71.3 percent—replied that they wanted to build additional wealth so they could give more meaningful support to charitable causes.

While individual, spontaneous donations to charity will always be gratefully accepted, proper planning will create more worth both for you and the causes you believe in and want to support. A charitable donation made from your income on the spur of the moment, as nice as it may be, is not a planned gift. Planned giving involves making significant charitable gifts part of an overall wealth-management strategy. Charitable giving can and should be coordinated with both estate and tax planning—two of the other five major concerns of affluent families—so that you as the donor, your family, and the charities you wish to support receive maximum benefit.

The tax code incorporates numerous provisions specifically designed to encourage planned charitable giving. In general, planned gifts provide not only income-tax deductions but estate-planning and capital gains-tax benefits.

Remember, however, that charity should take first place among these calculations. If your only concern is tax mitigation, other strategies will probably produce better results. However, if you genuinely care about supporting the charities and causes close to your heart, you should seriously consider planned giving as part of your overall wealth-management strategy. It's an effective way to do something worthwhile for others while also helping yourself—for, as was just said, doing well by doing good.

## BEQUESTS

The first step in planning is understanding what's possible. There are a number of different types of planned gifts, which fall into two general categories: bequests and foundations or funds. We'll deal with bequests first.

Bequests, which leave charitable gifts in your will, are the simplest and most common planned charitable gifts. One of the main advantages of this approach is simplicity: a bequest doesn't require much administrative oversight or other involvement during your lifetime. The assets you bequeath remain available to you in the meantime. When you pass away, your estate will be able to take a tax deduction for the amount of the bequest.

A more innovative variation of a bequest is a charitable gift of life insurance. As a donor, you can designate the charity of your choice to be the owner and beneficiary of a life insurance policy. This enables you to make a significant gift while taking tax deductions for the life insurance premiums.

A charitable-gift annuity is another variation on this theme, but one in which the bequest is made during your lifetime rather than upon your death. You and your qualified charity enter into a contract in which you receive an annuity or guaranteed lifetime income in exchange for your gift. There are three possible tax advantages to this approach: a modest income-tax deduction for the value of the gift, a reduction of capital gains tax if the gift consists of appreciated assets, and an estate-tax abatement.

## FOUNDATIONS, TRUSTS, AND SUPPORTING ORGANIZATIONS

Bequests are relatively straightforward. Charitable foundations and their cousins often involve creation of a legal charter and ongoing administration. However, such organizations give those who wish to give larger, ongoing charitable gifts the means to do so. Foundations and similar organizations can be lumped into two general categories: foundations or trusts involving a single affluent individual or family, and funds involving a number of individuals. We'll deal with single-family foundations and trusts first.

A private charitable foundation is a nonprofit organization that receives most of its contributions from a single affluent individual or family. It is established as a vehicle for distributing assets to a variety of charitable organizations and ventures, which the donor designates, and which may change over time. A minimum percentage of the foundation's assets must be distributed to legitimate charities each year. While this amount changes, currently the figure is about 5 percent. The remainder of the foundation's assets are usually invested, with the returns being retained by the foundation for its charitable work.

Another option is what's called a "supporting organization," which is very similar to a foundation except that its charitable beneficiaries are designated in advance. A supporting organization can be seen as a nonprofit that "supports" other specific charities. It is operated solely for their benefit, to help them carry out their work. Once a supporting organization is established and its beneficiaries are designated, those beneficiaries cannot be changed.

A third option is a charitable trust, which is similar to a charitable foundation in that it is generally established by a single affluent individual or family. However, as the name implies, the donations or assets involved are placed in a time-limited trust. There are two types of charitable trust that are structured in opposite but complementary ways: a charitable remainder trust and a charitable lead trust.

A charitable remainder trust delays the donation's benefit to charity. Income from the trust is reserved either for the donor or someone else the donor names, either for life or a specified number of years. At that point, the trust is dissolved, and its assets are distributed to the chosen charities.

A charitable lead trust works more or less the other way around. You, as donor, transfer assets to the trust for life or a specified number of years, and the trust's income is paid to your charity of choice. Once the trust expires, the assets are returned to you, your estate, or your heirs.

## FUNDS

Funds, in contrast to foundations, supporting organizations, and trusts, are entities that facilitate charitable contributions from a number of affluent individuals or families rather than a single donor. There are two different kinds of funds: the donor-advised fund and the pooled-income fund.

You can think of a donor-advised fund (DAF) as a charity that invests in pooled investment vehicles similar to mutual funds. You donate to the DAF, which is a nonprofit, and earn an income-tax deduction for the entire amount given. Later, whenever and at whatever pace you choose, you can decide which charities you want your donation to benefit, as well as how much of your original donation you want to give each charity. The DAF then sends a check to the charity or charities you've designated.

Pooled-income funds are another form of charitable mutual fund. The major difference between a pooled-income fund and a DAF is that the pooled fund pools donations from a number of donors for the benefit of a single, predetermined charity. As with most charitable vehicles, individual donations to the fund can be deducted from income taxes, and gifts of appreciated assets can be used to reduce capital gains taxes.

It's worth noting something of a generational shift here. In the past, extremely wealthy families tended to establish their own foundations, such as the Rockefeller and MacArthur Foundations. Funds, and DAFs in particular, have begun to find more favor with today's Rockefellers, such as Mark Zuckerberg and his wife, Priscilla Chan. Convenience is also a factor here. Donors generally do not establish or administer funds but use already established funds as a means to facilitate their charitable giving.

## SETTING A STRATEGY

As you can see, there are any number of options for planned charitable giving, just as there are many investment or tax-mitigation options. The number of moving parts and multiple goals involved can easily become confusing. What charities would you find it most meaningful to support? What other wealth-management strategies, such as tax and estate planning, can best be served by a well-thought-through charitable-giving plan?

As always, deciding which of these options is best for you and your family is done most effectively with the assistance of competent professionals. Specific concerns may differ, but the underlying point remains: The Household Endowment Model and its Wealth-Planning for Affluent Families have been developed to give you access to a coordinated network of expertise, including expert help in charitable giving.

One reason you work so hard is because you want to make a dent in the universe. Probably the best way to do so is to remember that charity—affluent families' fifth major concern—begins at home.

# CONCLUSION

Your money doesn't come with instructions. That's why this book was written—as a money manual to help you make a paradigm shift in how you look at all aspects of wealth management, starting with investment strategy. THEM—The Household Endowment Model—and its Wealth-Planning for Affluent Families are a new approach that can help affluent families and high-net-worth individuals—and those who aspire to this status—retain and grow their wealth.

It's quite surprising and even shocking how many affluent families lack a coordinated wealth-management strategy. It may be that business owners are so focused on growing their businesses that they don't feel they have the time to take a broader perspective. But that's no excuse. You wouldn't try to get to New York or LA by getting on the nearest freeway and then driving at random. If you want to get somewhere—in your car or with your finances—you've got to have a plan.

THEM provides such an integrated, coordinated plan, one that addresses all the five major concerns of affluent families: wealth preservation, wealth enhancement, wealth transfer, wealth protection, and charitable giving. Wealth preservation and investment counseling may be the cornerstone of this approach, but the THEM strategy encompasses the entire spectrum of concerns.

Let's take another look at the cornerstone—a radically new approach to investment that changes in the law have only made possible in recent years. Endowment-style investment, particularly in privately held assets, such as venture capital, private equity, and commercial real estate, not correlated with public markets, was once available only to large institutions and ultra-wealthy individuals. Now far more people can access and leverage these strategies at much more affordable buy-in rates.

This is news that has yet to reach most people who could profit from it. It also has yet to reach most of these people's investment counselors, who ought to know better but rarely do.

Now you know what they don't. You do not have to remain completely strapped to the public-market roller coaster and its precipitous ups and downs. Potentially, your new, institutional-style portfolio won't be subject to the kind of volatility that knocked so many people on their backs during the market meltdowns of 2000 and 2008–2009.

You now have access to what you need to escape the trap of outdated financial tradition: the THEM wealth-management network, consisting of a team of what we believe are some of the best-of-class professionals, including attorneys and accountants with in-depth specializations. Now you can have your own virtual family office without hiring a full-time cadre of financial, legal, and other experts at ruinous expense.

Once your new portfolio is in place, you and your wealth-management team can move on to your other major concerns: tax reduction and mitigation, which will enable you to retain and invest more of what you earn; estate planning to effectively transfer your wealth to your heirs just as you prefer; protection of your assets from lawsuits, creditors, and the other dangers lurking in the jungle out there; and, last but certainly not least, the charitable giving that will help you make a dent in the universe.

A balanced strategy requires coordination, which is the responsibility of the wealth manager sitting at the center of the network. If your wealth manager can save you 20 percent on your tax bill, you now have that much more net worth that you, with the help of your expert advisors, can invest and grow.

All this very good news is also very actionable. The Household Endowment Model is a new development built on years of experience. An expanding network of THEM advisors has now been trained in the model and its strategies.

Look at this from another angle. Financial success depends on three fundamental components:

- *Precision*: The degree of certainty that, within reason, you are or will be able to attain appropriate financial goals. Precision gives you *goals*.
- *Implementation*: The degree to which you are able to achieve your desired results. Implementation gives you *results*.
- *Access*: Your confidence that you will get the outcomes you want and need. Access gives you *confidence* in that you will achieve success.

Does your current financial plan cover and balance all three of these components? To find out, take the online financial stress test available at https://www.thehouseholdendowmentmodel.com/stress-test.

For more general information about The Household

Endowment Model, visit our website: https://www. thehouseholdendowmentmodel.com/.

Please also check out the podcast *Your Money Manual*, because, as we say, "when it comes to investing, your money doesn't come with instructions": https://www. thehouseholdendowmentmodel.com/podcast

Better still, to get further faster and to speak with us directly for additional education, contact us at The Household Endowment Model at 833-THEMUSA (833-843-6872).

If you've ever wondered whether there might be a better way to do what you've been trying to do for so many years, and if you're still not feeling like you're getting where you want to go, you'll find these next steps very worthwhile.

# RISK DISCLOSURE STATEMENT

THROUGHOUT THIS BOOK CONCEPTS HAVE BEEN DISCUSSED INCLUDING BUT NOT LIMITED TO GENERAL FINANCIAL, INVESTMENT, TAX, AND LEGAL STRATEGIES. THESE CONCEPTS AND STRATEGIES ARE NOT INTENDED TO PROVIDE THE BASIS OF A SPECIFIC RECOMMENDATION FOR YOUR PERSONAL SITUATION OR FUTURE FINANCIAL OR INVESTMENT DIRECTION. YOUR REVIEW OF THE CONTENT HEREIN AND FURTHER CONSULTATION WITH VARIOUS OTHER CONSULTANTS IS REQUIRED TO INFORM YOU AS TO HOW OUR FINANCIAL, INVESTMENT, TAX, OR LEGAL DISCUSSIONS MAY BE OF BENEFIT TO YOU AND YOUR FAMILY. PLEASE SEEK ADDITIONAL INFORMATION AND EDUCATION AS TO HOW THESE STRATEGIES MIGHT BE APPLIED TO YOUR SPECIFIC SITUATION FROM QUALIFIED PROFESSIONALS. PLEASE DO NOT CONSIDER ANY DISCUSSION OR RECOMMENDATIONS AS SPECIFIC INVESTMENT, TAX, OR LEGAL ADVICE.

# ACKNOWLEDGMENTS

I would like to acknowledge and thank these key strategic relationships for their contributions to, belief in, and support of The Household Endowment Model and its wealth-planning strategy. Please forgive me if I have inadvertently omitted any of my much-valued relationships. I am grateful to you all.

Jeff Allen, Robert Ambrosi, Todd Bailey, David Becker, Jake Bisenius, John Bowen, Paul Dietrich, Trent Erickson, Michael A. Freeman, Dana Goldstein, Francis J. Greenburger, Anthony Hazen, Michael Knapp, Matt Leiter, Arthur Levine, Paul Mason, Mark McCall, Clayton Mobley, Pat Murphy, Vali Nasr, Jonathan Powell, Russ Alan Prince, Michael P. Sealy, Jeffrey Sica, Michael Snyder, J. Alan Soelberg, James Steuterman, Jeff Stone, J. R. Thacker, Michael Weil, Carter Williams, and Rob Woomer.

# ABOUT THE AUTHOR

**VINCE ANNABLE** entered the financial services business in 1981 and created the Wealth Strategies Advisory Group in 2009. He's also the proud creator of The Household Endowment Model (THEM), an investment and wealth-planning platform that he created based on Yale University's successful endowment fund investment strategy and the elite wealth-planning strategies employed by other wealth-planning experts he has consulted with, including John Bowen and Russ Alan Prince.

Made in the USA
Columbia, SC
08 January 2020